Activities Manual/Study Guide

to accompany

Looking Out/ Looking In

SECOND CANADIAN EDITION

Ronald B. Adler
Neil Towne
Judith A. Rolls

Prepared by

Harry Havey
Red River College

Mary O. Wiemann
Santa Barbara City College

THOMSON

NELSON

Australia   Canada   Mexico   Singapore   Spain   United Kingdom   United States

THOMSON

✳ ™

NELSON

Activities Manual/Study Guide to accompany
Looking Out, Looking In, Second Canadian Edition,
by Ronald B. Adler, Neil Towne, and Judith A. Rolls
Prepared by Harry Havey and Mary O. Wiemann

Editorial Director and Publisher:
Evelyn Veitch

Acquisitions Editor:
Anne Williams

Marketing Manager:
Lenore Taylor

Senior Developmental Editor:
Rebecca Rea

Senior Production Editor:
Bob Kohlmeier

Production Coordinator:
Hedy Sellers

Creative Director:
Angela Cluer

Cover Design:
Johanna Liburd

Interior-Design Modifications:
Gerry Dunn

Compositor:
Gerry Dunn

Copy Editor:
Vivien Leong

Proofreader:
Jim Leahy

Printer:
Webcom

National Library of Canada Cataloguing in Publication

Havey, Harry
Activities manual/study guide to accompany Looking out/looking in, second Canadian edition / Harry Havey and Mary O. Wiemann.

ISBN 0-17-641628-5

1. Interpersonal communication— Problems, exercises, etc.
2. Interpersonal communication— Study and teaching (Higher)
I. Wiemann, Mary O.   II. Adler, Ronald B. (Ronald Brian), 1946–   .
Looking out/looking in.   III. Title.

BF637.C45A34 2003 Suppl. 1
158.2   C2003-903470-4

CONTENTS

Preface   ix

Chapter 1   **A First Look at Interpersonal Relationships   1**

OUTLINE 1

KEY TERMS 4

ACTIVITIES 7
- ◆   1.1   Communication Skills Inventory (Invitation to Insight)   7
- ◆   1.2   Expanding Your Communication Effectiveness (Invitation to Insight)   9
- ◆   1.3   Examining Your Own Messages across Dimensions (Skill Builder)   11

STUDY GUIDE 14

Crossword Puzzle   14
True/False   15
Completion   16
Multiple Choice 17

STUDY GUIDE ANSWERS 19

Chapter 2   **Communication and the Self   21**

OUTLINE 21

KEY TERMS 22

ACTIVITIES 25
- ◆   2.1   Who Do You Think You Are? (Invitation to Insight)   25
- ◆   2.2   Ego Boosters and Busters (Invitation to Insight)   27
- ◆   2.3   Self-Concept Inventory (Invitation to Insight)   31
- ◆❖ 2.4   Your Self-Fulfilling Prophecies (Skill Builder)   35
- ◆   2.5   Changing Your Self-Concept (Skill Builder)   39
- ◆   2.6   Your Public and Private Selves (Invitation to Insight)   43
- ◆❖ 2.7   What's in an Object? (Invitation to Insight)   45
- ❖   2.8   Mediated Messages – Identity Management (Group Discussion)   47

STUDY GUIDE 48

Crossword Puzzle   48
Matching   49

True/False 50
Completion 51
Multiple Choice 51

STUDY GUIDE ANSWERS 53

Chapter 3   Perception: What You See Is What You Get   55

OUTLINE 55

KEY TERMS 57

ACTIVITIES 59

◆   3.1   From Stereotypes to Empathy (Invitation to Insight)   59
◆   3.2   Exploring the Future (Invitation to Insight)   61
◆   3.3   Shifting Perspectives (Pillow Method) (Invitation to Insight)   63
❖   3.4   Observation and Perception (Skill Builder)   65
◆❖ 3.5   Applying Perception Checking (Skill Builder)   69
◆❖ 3.6   Perception-Checking Practice (Skill Builder)   75
❖   3.7   Perception Checking (Oral Skill)   79
◆❖ 3.8   Your Call – Perception (Group Discussion)   81

STUDY GUIDE 82

Crossword Puzzle   82
Matching   83
True/False   84
Completion   85
Multiple Choice   86

STUDY GUIDE ANSWERS 87

Chapter 4   Emotions: Thinking, Feeling, and Acting   89

OUTLINE 89

KEY TERMS 91

ACTIVITIES 93

◆❖ 4.1   Identifying Specific and Multiple Emotions (Skill Builder) 93
❖   4.2   Find the Feelings (Skill Builder)   95
❖   4.3   Stating Emotions Effectively (Skill Builder)   99
◆   4.4   Expressing Emotions Appropriately (Skill Builder)   101
◆   4.5   Disputing Irrational Thoughts (Invitation to Insight)   103
❖   4.6   Mediated Messages – Expressing Emotion (Group Discussion) 105
❖   4.7   Your Call – Expressing Emotion (Group Discussion) 107

STUDY GUIDE 109

Crossword Puzzle   109
True/False   110
Completion   111
Multiple Choice   111

STUDY GUIDE ANSWERS   114

Chapter 5   Language: Barrier and Bridge   115

OUTLINE   115

KEY TERMS   117

ACTIVITIES   121

- ❖ 5.1   Label the Language (Skill Builder)   121
- ❖ 5.2   Behavioural Descriptions (Skill Builder)   125
- ◆ 5.3   Language Clarity (Skill Builder)   127
- ◆❖ 5.4   Practising "I" Language (Skill Builder)   131
- ❖ 5.5   "I" Language (Oral Skill)   135
- ❖ 5.6   Mediated Messages – Language (Group Discussion)   137
- ❖ 5.7   Your Call – Language (Group Discussion)   139

STUDY GUIDE   140

Crossword Puzzle   140
Matching   141
True/False   142
Completion   143
Multiple Choice   143

STUDY GUIDE ANSWERS   145

Chapter 6   Nonverbal Communication: Messages without Words   147

OUTLINE   147

KEY TERMS   149

ACTIVITIES   151

- ❖ 6.1   Describing Nonverbal States (Skill Builder)   151
- ❖ 6.2   Nonverbal Complaints (Skill Builder)   153
- ❖ 6.3   Show and Tell (Skill Builder)   157
- ◆ 6.4   Evaluating Ambiguity (Invitation to Insight)   159
- ❖ 6.5   Mediated Messages – Nonverbal Communication (Group Discussion)   163
- ❖ 6.6   Your Call – Nonverbal Behaviour (Group Discussion)   165

STUDY GUIDE 166

Crossword Puzzle   166
True/False   167
Completion   168
Multiple Choice   168

STUDY GUIDE ANSWERS   170

Chapter 7   Listening: More Than Meets the Ear   173

OUTLINE   173

KEY TERMS   176

ACTIVITIES   177

◆   7.1   Listening Diary (Invitation to Insight)   177
❖   7.2   Responses to Problems (Skill Builder)   179
❖   7.3   Paraphrasing Practice (Skill Builder)   185
❖   7.4   Listening for Feelings (Skill Builder)   187
❖   7.5   Paraphrasing Information (Skill Builder)   189
❖   7.6   Listening and Responding Styles   191
◆   7.7   What Would You Say? Really! (Skill Builder)   193
❖   7.8   Mediated Messages – Listening (Group Discussion)   195
❖   7.9   Your Call – Listening (Group Discussion)   197

STUDY GUIDE   199

Crossword Puzzle   199
True/False   200
Completion   201
Multiple Choice   201

STUDY GUIDE ANSWERS   205

Chapter 8   Communication and Relational Dynamics   207

OUTLINE   207

KEY TERMS   210

ACTIVITIES   213

◆   8.1   Discovering Dialectics (Invitation to Insight)   213
◆   8.2   Breadth and Depth of Relationships (Invitation to Insight)   217
◆   8.3   Reasons for Nondisclosure (Invitation to Insight)   219
◆   8.4   Degrees of Self-Disclosure (Invitation to Insight)   221
❖   8.5   Responses in Relationships (Skill Builder)   225
❖   8.6   Relational Stages and Self-Disclosure (Skill Builder)   231

❖   8.7   The Interview (Invitation to Insight)   235
❖   8.8   Mediated Messages – Relational Dynamics (Group Discussion)   237
❖   8.9   Your Call – Relational Dynamics (Group Discussion)   239

STUDY GUIDE   241

Crossword Puzzle   241
Matching   242
True/False   243
Completion   244
Multiple Choice   245

STUDY GUIDE ANSWERS   246

Chapter 9   Improving Communication Climates   249

OUTLINE   249

KEY TERMS   250

ACTIVITIES   253

◆   9.1   Understanding Your Defensive Responses (Invitation to Insight) 253
◆❖ 9.2   Defensive and Supportive Language (Skill Builder)   257
❖   9.3   Coping with Typical Criticism (Skill Builder)   261
❖   9.4   Responding Nondefensively (Oral Skill)   263
❖   9.5   Mediated Messages – Climate (Group Discussion)   265
❖   9.6   Your Call – Climate (Group Discussion)   267

STUDY GUIDE   268

Crossword Puzzle   268
True/False 269
Completion   270
Multiple Choice 271
Study Guide Answers   273

Chapter 10   Managing Interpersonal Conflicts   275

OUTLINE   275

KEY TERMS   277

ACTIVITIES   279

◆❖ 10.1 Understanding Conflict Styles (Skill Builder)   279
◆❖ 10.2 Writing Clear Messages (Skill Builder)   285
◆   10.3 Your Conflict Styles (Invitation to Insight)   289

◆❖ 10.4 The Ends vs. the Means (Invitation to Insight) 293

◆❖ 10.5 Win–Win Problem Solving (Invitation to Insight) 297

❖   10.6 Conflict Resolution Dyads (Oral Skill) 301

❖   10.7 Mediated Messages – Conflict Management (Group Discussion) 303

❖   10.8 Your Call – Conflict Management (Group Discussion) 305

STUDY GUIDE 306

Crossword Puzzle 306
True/False 307
Completion 308
Multiple Choice 309

STUDY GUIDE ANSWERS 311

PREFACE

Welcome to the *Activities Manual/Study Guide* for *Looking Out/Looking In*, Second Canadian Edition. This Activities Manual/Study Guide is designed to enhance student learning. It contains more than 50 class-tested exercises and more than 500 study test items designed to build understanding of principles and proficiency in skills introduced in the text.

Each chapter in the *Activities Manual/Study Guide* parallels the chapter in *Looking Out/Looking In*. The following areas in each chapter combine to provide a thorough, student-centred learning package:

- **Outlines** Extended outlines of each chapter begin each section. Many instructors ask students to use the outlines as a lecture guide in class or a place to take notes as they read the chapter.

- **Key Terms** Vocabulary terms for each chapter follow the outlines; they are spaced so that students can write in definitions for each term in the *Study Guide*. This helps students study for exams and focus on important concepts.

- **Activities** Students who complete the activities in this manual will develop understanding and skill in each area through a choice of exercises. Exercises are coded with icons to help one choose how to use them: ❖ denotes a group activity; ◆ identifies an individual activity.

    Skill Builder activities – designed primarily to help students identify the target behaviour in a number of common interpersonal communication situations. These are frequently group activities that reinforce learning in the classroom. They can be done as individual activities.

    Invitation to Insight activities – designed to help students discover how newly learned principles can be applied in their everyday lives. They can be grouped together to form a "communication journal" for the entire course. While these activities are usually designed for individual use, they can provide the structure for small group discussion or lecture/discussion.

    Oral Skill activities – designed to allow students to actually exhibit communication behaviours they have studied. They are designed for dyadic or small group use in a classroom or lab setting.

    Mediated Communication activities – designed to challenge students to apply interpersonal communication principles to the many mediated contexts they encounter. they are designed for dyadic or small group use in a classroom or lab setting

    Your Call activities – designed to prompt analysis and ethical choices among students. They are designed primarily for group discussion in a classroom or lab setting.

- **Study Guide** The activities here will help students identify major concepts or skills contained in the chapter. The Crossword Puzzle, Matching, True/False, Completion, and Multiple Choice items are designed to be done individually, in groups, or with the entire class; answer keys can be found at the end of each chapter. The exercises provide a review and reinforcement for students as they work at their own pace.

Many of the activities can be used in a variety of ways. Instructors can adapt them, use some or all, grade them or leave them ungraded, assign them as out-of-class exercises, or use them as class enrichment. Student observations in many exercises will lead to class discussions on how to apply the newly learned principles in the "real world" of one's interpersonal relationships.

While they almost always stimulate class discussion, the activities in this manual are designed to do more than keep a class busy or interested. If they are used regularly, they will help students to move beyond simply understanding the principles of interpersonal communication and actually to perform more effectively in a variety of communication situations.

The *Activities Manual/Study Guide* should help develop more effective communication, both in class and in students' lives outside the classroom. Students who go through the outlines, fill in the key terms, and complete the study guides do better on quizzes and tests than those who fail to complete some or all of these aids. The greatest satisfaction, however, comes from using the activities in this manual to develop more effective communication with loved ones, co-workers, and friends.

Mary O. Wiemann
Harry Havey

CHAPTER 1

A First Look at Interpersonal Relationships

OUTLINE

Use this outline to take notes as you read the chapter in the text and/or as your instructor lectures in class.

I. Introduction to interpersonal communication

    A. Communication Is Important

    B. Why We Communicate

        1. Physical needs

        2. Identity needs

        3. Social needs

            a. Pleasure

            b. Affection

            c. Inclusion

            d. Escape

            e. Relaxation

            f. Control

        4. Practical goals

            a. Instrumental goals

            b. Maslow's basic needs

                1) Physical

                2) Safety

                3) Social

                4) Self-esteem

                5) Self-actualization

II. The process of communication

    A. A Linear View

        1. Sender

        2. Encoding

       3. Message

       4. Channel

       5. Decoding

       6. Receiver

       7. Noise

          a. External (physical)

          b. Physiological

          c. Psychological

       8. Environments

   B. **A Transactional View**

       1. Feedback is verbal and nonverbal

       2. We send/receive messages simultaneously

       3. Nonisolated "acts" are involved

       4. Behaviours are verbal and nonverbal

III.   Communication principles and misconceptions

   A. **Communication Principles**

       1. Communication can be intentional or unintentional

       2. It's impossible not to communicate

       3. Communication is irreversible

       4. Communication is unrepeatable

   B. **Avoiding Communication Misconceptions**

       1. Meanings are not in words

       2. More communication is not always better

       3. No single person or event causes another's reaction

       4. Communication will not solve all problems

       5. Communication is not a natural ability

IV.   The nature of interpersonal communication

   A. **Two Views of Interpersonal Communication**

       1. Quantitative – dyadic

       2. Qualitative

          a. Uniqueness

          b. Irreplaceability

          c. Interdependence

          d. Disclosure

   B. **Personal and Impersonal Communication: A Matter of Balance**

   C. **Technology and Interpersonal Communication**

V.   Communicating about relationships

   A. **Content and Relational Messages**

   B. **Metacommunication**

   C. **Types of Relational Messages**

       1. Affinity

       2. Respect

NAME _____

ACTIVITIES

1.1   COMMUNICATION SKILLS INVENTORY

◆ Activity Type: Invitation to Insight

PURPOSES

1. To help you discover how satisfied you are with the way you communicate in various situations.
2. To preview some topics that will be covered in *Looking Out/Looking In.*

INSTRUCTIONS

1. Below you will find several communication-related situations. As you read each item, imagine yourself in that situation.
2. For each instance, answer the following question: *How satisfied am I with the way I would behave in this situation and ones like it?* You can express your answers by placing one of the following numbers in the space by each item:

   5 = Completely satisfied with my probable action
   4 = Generally, though not totally, satisfied with my probable action
   3 = About equally satisfied and dissatisfied with my probable action
   2 = Generally, though not totally, dissatisfied with my probable action
   1 = Totally dissatisfied with my probable action

_____ **1.** A new acquaintance has just shared some personal experiences with you that make you think you'd like to develop a closer relationship. You have experienced the same things and are now deciding whether to reveal these personal experiences. (8)

_____ **2.** You've become involved in a political discussion with someone whose views are the complete opposite of yours. The other person asks, "Can't you at least understand why I feel as I do?" (3, 7)

_____ **3.** You are considered a responsible adult by virtually everyone except one relative who still wants to help you make all your decisions. You value your relationship with this person, but you need to be seen as more independent. You know you should do something about this situation. (9, 10)

_____ **4.** In a mood of self-improvement a friend asks you to describe the one or two ways by which you think he or she could behave better. You're willing to do so, but need to express yourself in a clear and helpful way. (3, 5, 10)

_____ **5.** A close companion says that you've been behaving "differently" lately and asks if you know what he or she means. (5, 6, 7)

_____ **6.** You've grown to appreciate a new friend a great deal lately, and you realize that you ought to share your feelings. (4)

_____ **7.** An amateur writer you know has just shown you his or her latest batch of poems and asked your opinion of them. You don't think they are very good. It's time for your reply. (5, 9, 10)

_____ **8.** You've found certain behaviours of an important person in your life have become more and more bothersome to you. It's getting harder to keep your feelings to yourself. (4, 10)

_____ **9.** You're invited to a party at which everyone except the host will be a stranger to you. Upon hearing about this, a friend says, "Gee, if I were going I'd feel like an outsider. They probably won't have much to do with you." How do you feel? (2)

_____ **10.** A friend comes to you feeling very upset about a recent incident and asks for advice. You suspect that there is more to the problem than just this one incident. You really want to help the friend. (7)

_____ **11.** You find yourself defending the behaviour of a friend against the criticisms of a third person. The critic accuses you of seeing only what you want to see and ignoring the rest. (2, 4, 5, 9, 10)

_____ **12.** A boss or instructor asks you to explain a recent assignment to a companion who has been absent. You are cautioned to explain the work clearly so there will be no misunderstandings. (5)

_____ **13.** You ask an acquaintance for help with a problem. She says yes, but the way the message is expressed leaves you thinking she'd rather not. You do need the help, but only if it's sincerely offered. (6, 10)

_____ **14.** A roommate always seems to be too busy to do the dishes when it's his or her turn, and you've wound up doing them most of the time. You resent the unequal sharing of responsibility and want to do something about it. (10)

_____ **15.** A new acquaintance has become quite interested in getting to know you better, but you feel no interest yourself. You've heard that this person is extremely sensitive and insecure. (1, 2)

Parenthetical numbers following each item indicate the chapters of _Looking Out/Looking In_ which focus on that subject.

You can use the results of this survey in two ways. By looking at each question you can see how satisfied you are with your behaviour in that specific type of situation. A response of 1 or 2 on any single question is an obvious signal that you can profit from working on that situation.

By totalling your score for all of the items you can get an idea of how satisfied you are with your overall ability to communicate in interpersonal situations. A score of 68–75 suggests high satisfaction, 58–67 indicates moderate satisfaction, while 45–57 shows that you feel dissatisfied with your communication behaviours nearly half the time.

Another valuable way to use this activity is to make a second inventory at the end of the course. Have you improved? Are there still areas you will need to work on?

NAME _____

1.2   EXPANDING YOUR COMMUNICATION EFFECTIVENESS

◆ Activity Type: Invitation to Insight

PURPOSES

1. To help you broaden your repertoire of effective communication behaviours and your skill at performing them.
2. To help you identify the most appropriate communication behaviours in important situations.

INSTRUCTIONS

1. Use the space below to identify two areas in which you would like to communicate more effectively.
2. For each area, identify a person you have observed who communicates in a way that you think would improve your effectiveness. Describe this person's communication behaviour.
3. Describe how you could adapt these behaviours to your own life.

EXAMPLE

A. Area in which you would like to communicate more effectively *Making conversation with people I've just met.*
B. Model who communicates effectively in this area *My friend Rich.*
C. Model's behaviour *He asks sincere questions of people he's just met, compliments them enthusiastically, and smiles a lot.*
D. How could you apply these behaviours? *I can spend more time thinking about people I've just met and less time thinking self-consciously about my own nervousness. Then I can focus on parts of these new people that interest me and let the other person know I'm interested. The key seems to be sincerity: I have to really mean what I say and not use questions and compliments as tricks.*

SITUATION 1

A. Area in which you would like to communicate more effectively_____

_____

B. Model who communicates effectively in this area _____

C. Model's behaviour _____

_____

D.   How could you apply these behaviours? _____

_____

_____

SITUATION 2

A.   Area in which you would like to communicate more effectively_____

_____

B.   Model who communicates effectively in this area_____

C.   Model's behaviour _____

_____

D.   How could you apply these behaviours? _____

_____

_____

_____

NAME _____

1.3   EXAMINING YOUR OWN MESSAGES ACROSS DIMENSIONS

◆ ACTIVITY TYPE : SKILL BUILDER

PURPOSES
1. To recognize that messages have several dimensions
2. To examine your own messages for multiple dimensions

INSTRUCTIONS
1. Look over the example provided below
2. Record and examine two examples of communication that you initiated. Have one example involving a friend or acquaintance and the second example involving a relative stranger (e.g., a store clerk at Canadian Tire).

EXAMPLE
Description of the situation – You disagree with your instructor about whether the testing and grading system is fair. You have tried to have a discussion with her about this but so far she has been unable to find the time.

Examination

A. Relational levels (inclusion, control, affection, respect)
   I think I just want more control over the evaluation methods so that they reflect my own preferences or strengths and because I can't see how they relate to the course objectives. My instructor's inability to find time may reflect a lack of respect for my opinions or, depending on how I expressed myself, a perception that I don't respect her.

B. Communication needs (physical, identity, social) and practical goals (instrumental)
   I think that I initiated this communication in order to get an instrumental goal met – to get the course evaluation changed. But I think I may also have some identity needs too – what does the instructor think of me?

C. Impersonal and interpersonal communication
   I think this is more impersonal communication – the course has just started and I don't know the instructor well enough to know how to approach her so the communication is pretty formal at this point. I'm certainly dependent on her (interpersonal) but I'm not sure if the feeling is mutual. I don't think she even realizes how much this issue means to me.

D. Is this an example of metacommunication?
   No – I definitely have some feelings about how we're communicating (or not communicating) about this issue but I certainly haven't mentioned them to her, nor she to me.

E.   Becoming a more competent communicator
I think I may need to become more assertive about having a meeting. At the same time, I'll watch that my communication stays as respectful as possible. I think that I'll monitor my interaction style pretty closely for the next while and try to keep in mind that this isn't the only course she teaches and she may not have much free time right now. But I am serious about this and I do want her to know why.

Your Situation Involving a Friend or Acquaintance

Description of the situation:

_____

_____

_____

_____

A.   Relational levels (inclusion, control, affection, respect)

_____

_____

_____

_____

B.   Communication needs (physical, identity, social) and practical goals (instrumental)

_____

_____

_____

_____

C.   Impersonal and interpersonal communication

_____

_____

_____

_____

D.   Is this an example of metacommunication?

_____

_____

_____

_____

E.   Becoming a more competent communicator

_____

_____

_____

_____

Your Situation Involving a Relative Stranger

Description of the situation:

_____

_____

_____

_____

A. Relational levels (inclusion, control, affection, respect)

_____

_____

_____

_____

B. Communication needs (physical, identity, social) and practical goals (instrumental)

_____

_____

_____

_____

C. Impersonal and interpersonal communication

_____

_____

_____

_____

D. Is this an example of metacommunication?

_____

_____

_____

_____

E. Becoming a more competent communicator

_____

_____

_____

_____

STUDY GUIDE

CROSSWORD PUZZLE

Across

1 the social need to care for others and to be cared for by them

4 two individuals communicating

5 when the communication goal is to get someone to do what you want

6 the field of experiences that leads a person to make sense of another's behaviour

9 communication as a one-way event

10 the discernible response of a receiver to a sender's message

14 behaviour that treats others as objects rather than as individuals

15 one who notices and attends to a message

Down

1 the degree to which people like to appreciate each other

2 the medium through which a message passes from sender to receiver

3 any force that interferes with effective communication

4 the process during which a receiver attaches meaning to a message

7 communication in which the parties consider one another as unique individuals rather than as objects

8 the process of putting thoughts into symbols, most commonly words

10 the communication ability to accomplish one's personal goals in a manner that maintains a relationship on terms that are acceptable to all parties

11 the social need to influence others

12 the creator of a message

16 the social need being met when communication is used as a way to avoid unpleasant tasks

9. _____ is the process of paying close attention to your behaviour in order to shape the way you behave.

10. _____ is the ability to take the other person's perspective in a relationship.

MULTIPLE CHOICE

Choose the letter of the communication process element that is most illustrated by the description found below. Italicized words provide clues.

a. encode
b. decode
c. channel
d. message/feedback
e. noise (external, physiological, or psychological)
f. environment

_____ **1.** The children make a *videotape* of themselves to send to their grandparents instead of writing a *letter*.

_____ **2.** Lise tries to decide the best way to tell Johan that she can't go to Vancouver with him.

_____ **3.** Johan decides Lise means she doesn't love him when she says she can't go to Vancouver.

_____ **4.** The sound of the cooling fan in the overhead projector makes it difficult to concentrate on what the instructor's saying.

_____ **5.** Camille *smiles* while Elvis is talking to her.

_____ **6.** Brooke is daydreaming about her date while Allison is talking to her.

_____ **7.** Since Jacob has never been married, it's difficult for him to understand why his married friend Denis wants to spend less time with him.

_____ **8.** Whitney says, *"I'm positive about my vote."*

_____ **9.** Olivier *thinks* Joel wants to leave when he waves to him.

_____ **10.** Su Mei *winks* when she *says* she's serious and *gestures* with her arms.

_____ **11.** Erin is from a wealthy family and Kate from a poor one. They have a serious conflict about how to budget their money.

_____ **12.** Jacques has been feeling a cold coming on all day while he sat through the meeting.

_____ **13.** Levi constructs the best arguments to convince his parents to buy him a new car.

_____ **14.** Ilona decides to lie to her group members about the reason she missed the meeting last night.

_____ **15.** "I refuse to go," said Karim.

Choose the *best* answer for each of the questions below.

16. According to a contextual definition of interpersonal communication, interpersonal communication occurs when

    a. two people interact with one another, usually face to face.
    b. you watch a TV show about relationships.
    c. you read a romance novel.
    d. your romantic partner leaves a message on your answering machine.

17. All of the following statements are true *except*

    a. Communication can be intentional.
    b. Communication is irreversible.
    c. Communication can be unintentional.
    d. Communication is repeatable.

18. All of the following elements are included in the transactional communication model *except*

    a. sender.
    b. channel.
    c. complementarity.
    d. encoding.

19. The messages people exchange about their communication are termed

    a. affinity.
    b. metacommunication.
    c. complementary symmetry.
    d. communication competence.

20. When you notice that you are really starting to get the hang of a new communication technique, you have entered the skill stage of

    a. awareness.
    b. integration.
    c. awkwardness.
    d. skillfulness.

21. All of the following are examples of feedback *except*

    a. silence.
    b. a wink of an eye.
    c. a nasty thought.
    d. a frown.

22. All the following are areas of social need that we attempt to meet through communication *except*

    a. relaxation.
    b. escape.
    c. affection.
    d. conclusion.
    e. pleasure.

STUDY GUIDE ANSWERS

CROSSWORD PUZZLE

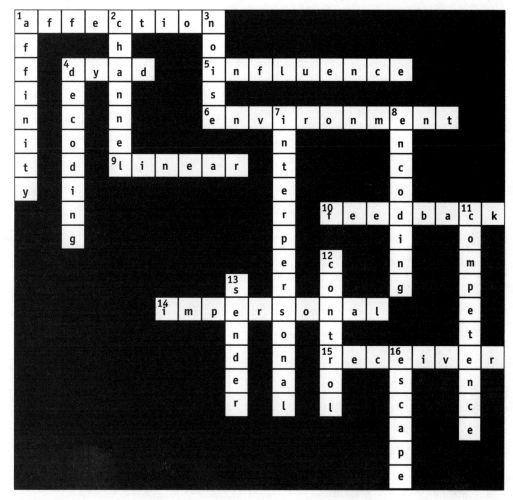

TRUE/FALSE

1. T	**4.** F	**7.** F	**10.** T	**13.** F
2. F	**5.** T	**8.** T	**11.** T	**14.** F
3. F	**6.** T	**9.** T	**12.** F	**15.** F

COMPLETION

1. identity needs
2. social needs
3. decoding
4. metacommunication
5. physiological noise
6. control
7. external noise
8. cognitive complexity
9. self-monitoring
10. empathy

MULTIPLE CHOICE

1. c	**5.** d	**9.** b	**13.** a	**17.** d	**21.** c
2. a	**6.** e	**10.** c	**14.** a	**18.** c	**22.** d
3. b	**7.** f	**11.** f	**15.** d	**19.** b	
4. e	**8.** d	**12.** e	**16.** a	**20.** d	

CHAPTER 2

Communication and the Self

OUTLINE

Use this outline to take notes as you read the chapter in the text and/or as your instructor lectures in class.

I. Communication and the self-concept

    A. Definition: The Relatively Stable Set of Perceptions You Hold of Yourself

    B. How the Self-Concept Develops
        1. Reflected appraisal (through significant others)
        2. Social comparison (through reference groups)

    C. Characteristics of the Self-Concept
        1. The self-concept is subjective
            a. Obsolete information
            b. Distorted feedback
            c. Emphasis on perfection
            d. Social expectations
        2. The self-concept resists change
            a. Change-not-acknowledged problem
            b. Self-delusion/lack of growth problem

    D. Influences on Identity
        1. Diversity
        2. Culture
        3. Sex and gender

    E. The Self-Fulfilling Prophecy and Communication
        1. Definition: Expectations held that make an outcome more likely
        2. Types
            a. Self-imposed
            b. Other-imposed
        3. Influence
            a. Improve relationships
            b. Damage relationships

F. **Changing Your Self-Concept**
1. Have realistic expectations
2. Have realistic perceptions
3. Have the will to change
4. Have the skill to change

II.   Presenting the self: Communication as identity management

A. **Public and Private Selves**
1. Perceived self
2. Presenting self

B. **Characteristics of Identity Management**
1. We strive to construct multiple identities
2. Identity management is collaborative
3. Identity management can be deliberate or unconscious
4. Identity management varies by situation
5. People differ in their degree of identity management

C. **Why Manage Identities?**
1. Social rules
2. Personal goals
3. Relational goals

D. **How Do We Manage Identities?**
1. Face-to-face
    a. Manner
    b. Appearance
2. Mediated

E. **Identity Management and Honesty**

KEY TERMS

Use these key terms to review major concepts from your text. Write the definition for each key term in the space to the right.

appearance _____

cognitive conservatism _____

collective identity _____

distorted feedback _____

ego booster _____

ego buster _____

face _____

front _____

identity management _____

individualistic identity _____

manner _____

myth of perfection _____

obsolete information _____

perceived self _____

presenting self _____

reference groups _____

reflected appraisal _____

self-concept _____

self-fulfilling prophecy _____

self-monitor _____

self-verification _____

setting _____

significant other _____

social comparison _____

social expectations _____

NAME _____

ACTIVITIES

2.1   WHO DO YOU THINK YOU ARE?

◆ Activity Type: Invitation to Insight

PURPOSE
To help you identify your own self-concept.

INSTRUCTIONS
1. For each category below, supply the words or phrases that describe you best.
2. After filling in the spaces within each category, organize your responses so that the most fundamental characteristic is listed first, with the rest of the items following in order of descending importance.

PART A: IDENTIFY THE ELEMENTS OF YOUR SELF-CONCEPT

1. What moods or feelings best characterize you (cheerful, considerate, optimistic, etc.)?

   a. _____   b. _____   c. _____

2. How would you describe your physical condition and/or your appearance (tall, attractive, weak, muscular, etc.)?

   a. _____   b. _____   c. _____

3. How would you describe your social traits (friendly, shy, aloof, talkative, etc.)?

   a. _____   b. _____   c. _____

4. What talents do you possess or lack (good artist, lousy carpenter, competent swimmer, etc.)?

   a. _____   b. _____   c. _____

5. How would you describe your intellectual capacity (curious, poor reader, good mathematician, etc.)?

   a. _____   b. _____   c. _____

6. What beliefs do you hold strongly (vegetarian, liberal, passivist, etc.)?

   a. _____   b. _____   c. _____

7. What social roles are the most important in your life (brother, student, friend, bank teller, club president, etc.)?

    a. _____   b. _____   c. _____

8. What other terms haven't you listed so far that describe other important things about yourself?

    a. _____   b. _____   c. _____

PART B: ARRANGE YOUR SELF-CONCEPT ELEMENTS IN ORDER OF IMPORTANCE

1. _____	13. _____
2. _____	14. _____
3. _____	15. _____
4. _____	16. _____
5. _____	17. _____
6. _____	18. _____
7. _____	19. _____
8. _____	20. _____
9. _____	21. _____
10. _____	22. _____
11. _____	23. _____
12. _____	24. _____

NOTE: You will use these descriptors in Activity 2.3.

NAME _____

2.2   EGO BOOSTERS AND BUSTERS

◆ Activity Type: Invitation to Insight

PURPOSES

1. To help you identify how significant others have shaped your self-concept.
2. To help you realize how you shape the self-concept of others.

INSTRUCTIONS

1. In the appropriate spaces below, describe the actions of several "ego boosters" – significant others who shaped your self-concept in a positive way. Also describe the behaviour of "ego busters" who contributed to a more negative self-concept.
2. Next, recall several incidents in which you behaved as an ego booster or buster to others. Not all ego boosters and busters are obvious. Include in your description several incidents in which the messages were subtle or nonverbal.
3. Summarize the lessons you have learned from this experience by answering the questions at the end of this exercise.

EGO BOOSTER MESSAGES YOU HAVE RECEIVED

EXAMPLE

I perceive(d) _my chem. lab partner_ as telling me I am/was _attractive_ when he
        (significant other)   (self-concept element)

or she _keeps (kept) sneaking glances at me and smiling during our experiments._

1. I perceive(d) _____ as telling me I am/was
                               (significant other)

_____ when he/she _____
    (self-concept element)

_____

_____

_____

2. I perceive(d) _____ as telling me I am/was
                               (significant other)

_____ when he/she _____
    (self-concept element)

_____

_____

_____

3. I perceive(d) _____ as telling me I am/was
                          (significant other)

_____ when he/she _____
        (self-concept element)

_____

_____

EGO BUSTER MESSAGES YOU HAVE RECEIVED

EXAMPLE

I perceive(d) _*my neighbour*_ as telling me I am/was _*not an important friend*_ when
                (significant other)   (self-concept element)

he/she *had a big party last weekend and didn't invite me.* _____

1. I perceive(d) _____ as telling me I am/was
                          (significant other)

_____ when he/she _____
        (self-concept element)

_____

_____

2. I perceive(d) _____ as telling me I am/was
                          (significant other)

_____ when he/she _____
        (self-concept element)

_____

_____

3. I perceive(d) _____ as telling me I am/was
                          (significant other)

_____ when he/she _____
        (self-concept element)

_____

_____

EGO BOOSTER MESSAGES YOU HAVE SENT

EXAMPLE

I was a booster to *my instructor* when I *told her I enjoyed last Tuesday's lecture.*

1. I was a booster to _____ when I _____

_____

_____

2. I was a booster to _____ when I _____

_____

_____

3. I was a booster to _____ when I _____

_____

_____

EGO BUSTER MESSAGES YOU HAVE SENT

EXAMPLE

I was a buster to *my sister* when I *forgot to phone her or send even a card on her*

birthday.

1. I was a buster to _____ when I _____

_____

2. I was a buster to _____ when I _____

_____

_____

3. I was a buster to _____ when I _____

_____

_____

CONCLUSIONS (USE AN ADDITIONAL SHEET OF PAPER IF NECESSARY)

Who are the people who have most influenced your self-concept in the past? What messages did each one send to influence you so strongly?

_____

_____

_____

_____

What people are the greatest influences on your self-concept now? Is each person a positive or a negative influence? What messages does each one send to influence your self-concept?

_____

_____

_____

_____

Who are the people whom _you_ have influenced most greatly? What messages have you sent to each one about his or her self-concept? How have you sent these messages?

_____

_____

_____

_____

What ego booster or buster messages do you want to send to the important people in your life? How can you send each one?

_____

_____

_____

_____

NAME _____

2.3   SELF-CONCEPT INVENTORY

◆ Activity Type: Invitation to Insight

PURPOSES

1. To give you a clearer picture of how you see yourself (your perceived self).
2. To illustrate how others perceive you (presenting self).

INSTRUCTIONS

1. Transfer the list of 24 elements of your self-concept from Activity 2.1 to index cards (or strips of paper). If you didn't do Activity 2.1, go back and complete that now.
2. Arrange your cards in a stack, with the one that *best* describes you at the top and the one that *least* describes you at the bottom.
3. Using the Perceived Self column (Table 1), record the order in which you arranged the cards (1 is the most like you). Continue your list on the next page.
4. Cover your Perceived Self column and ask two other people (a friend, co-worker, roommate, family member, classmate) to arrange the descriptors in an order in which they see you. Record these perceptions in Tables 2 and 3, being sure to cover your own Table 1 and the Table 2 or 3 that the other person has worked on (so no one sees what the other has written). Record the name/relationship of your evaluator at the top of the appropriate column.
5. Compare the three tables, circling any descriptors that differ from column to column.
6. Answer the questions at the end of this exercise.

TABLE 1 PERCEIVED SELF	TABLE 2 PRESENTING SELF TO	TABLE 3 PRESENTING SELF TO
	_____ (RELATIONSHIP TO YOU)	_____ (RELATIONSHIP TO YOU)
1. _____	1. _____	1. _____
2. _____	2. _____	2. _____
3. _____	3. _____	3. _____
4. _____	4. _____	4. _____
5. _____	5. _____	5. _____

TABLE 1 PERCEIVED SELF	TABLE 2 PRESENTING SELF TO	TABLE 3 PRESENTING SELF TO
	(RELATIONSHIP TO YOU)	(RELATIONSHIP TO YOU)
6. _____	6. _____	6. _____
7. _____	7. _____	7. _____
8. _____	8. _____	8. _____
9. _____	9. _____	9. _____
10. _____	10. _____	10. _____
11. _____	11. _____	11. _____
12. _____	12. _____	12. _____
13. _____	13. _____	13. _____
14. _____	14. _____	14. _____
15. _____	15. _____	15. _____
16. _____	16. _____	16. _____
17. _____	17. _____	17. _____
18. _____	18. _____	18. _____
19. _____	19. _____	19. _____
20. _____	20. _____	20. _____
21. _____	21. _____	21. _____
22. _____	22. _____	22. _____
23. _____	23. _____	23. _____
24. _____	24. _____	24. _____

Describe any factors that have contributed in a positive or negative way to the formation of your perceived self (obsolete information, social expectations, perfectionistic beliefs). Include any other factors involved in the formation of your perceived self (for example, certain significant others, any strong reference groups).

_____

_____

_____

_____

Describe any differences between your perceived self and the ways your evaluators perceived you (your presenting selves). What factors contribute to the differences in perception? Whose view is the most accurate and why?

_____

_____

_____

_____

_____

Why might your partners in this exercise view you differently from the way you perceive yourself? Would other people in your life view you like either of the people in this exercise? Give some specific examples with reasons why they would or would not have a similar perception.

_____

_____

_____

_____

_____

NAME _____

2.4   YOUR SELF-FULFILLING PROPHECIES

◆❖ Activity Type: Skill Builder

PURPOSES

1. To help you identify the self-fulfilling prophecies you impose on yourself.
2. To help you identify the self-fulfilling prophecies others impose on you.

INSTRUCTIONS

1. Identify three communication-related, self-fulfilling prophecies you impose on yourself. For each, identify the item, describe the prediction you make, and show how this prediction influences either your behaviour or that of others.
2. Next, identify two communication-related, self-fulfilling prophecies others have imposed on you. For each, show how the other person's prediction affected your behaviour.

PROPHECIES YOU IMPOSE ON YOURSELF

EXAMPLE

Item *Inept in social situations*
Prediction *When I'm at a party or other social gathering, I think about how foolish I'll sound when I meet strangers.*
Outcome *I do sound foolish when I meet them. I stammer, avoid eye contact, and can't think of anything interesting to say.*
How your prediction affected outcome *I think that expecting to fail causes me to sound foolish. If I didn't expect to sound so foolish, I'd probably behave with more confidence.*

1. Item _____

   Prediction _____

   _____

   _____

   Outcome _____

   _____

   _____

How prediction affected outcome _____

_____

_____

2. Item _____

Prediction _____

_____

_____

Outcome _____

_____

_____

How prediction affected outcome _____

_____

_____

3. Item _____

Prediction _____

_____

_____

Outcome _____

_____

_____

How prediction affected outcome _____

_____

_____

PROPHECIES OTHERS IMPOSE ON YOU

EXAMPLE
Item *Good listener*
Prediction *My friends often share their problems with me and tell me that I'm a good listener.*
Outcome *I'm willing to listen in the future.*
How your prediction affected outcome *Being told I'm a good listener makes me more willing to lend an ear. If they told me I was no help, I'd probably discourage them from bringing me their problems in the future.*

1. Item _____

Prediction _____

_____

_____

Outcome _____

_____

_____

How prediction affected outcome _____

_____

_____

2. Item _____

Prediction _____

_____

_____

Outcome _____

_____

_____

How prediction affected outcome _____

_____

_____

NAME _____

2.5   CHANGING YOUR SELF-CONCEPT

◆ Activity Type: Skill Builder

PURPOSE
To help you plan a course of action for two areas of your self-concept that you are committed to changing.

INSTRUCTIONS
Complete the following questionnaire.

EXAMPLE
A.   Identify an area of your self-concept that you'd like to change.
I'd like to see myself as a good student.

B.   Who would be a role model in this area – someone you could learn from through direct observation?
Melissa, who takes several of the same courses with me.

C.   What abilities or qualities that you would like to acquire does the model possess in this area?
She always seems so on top of her work and she's always ready for class.

D.   What would be a reasonable amount of improvement to achieve in the area you picked?
To be up-to-date on all the readings and assignments in at least two courses.

E.   Who would be a person you can trust to seek balanced feedback from?
My instructor has lots of opportunity to observe students dealing with workload pressures, and he always seems very fair and honest in his comments about things.

F.   Are there courses or resources that you could access to learn specific techniques in this area?
There are a few videos in the library on public speaking that I could watch.

G.   What will be your first step?
I think I'll go talk to my instructor to let him know what I'm working on and ask for feedback.

AREA 1

A. Identify an area of your self-concept that you'd like to change.

_____

_____

_____

B. Who would be a role model in this area – someone you could learn from through direct observation?

_____

_____

_____

C. What abilities or qualities that you would like to acquire does the model possess in this area?

_____

_____

_____

D. What would be a reasonable amount of improvement to achieve in the area you picked?

_____

_____

_____

E. Who would be a person you can trust to seek balanced feedback from?

_____

_____

_____

F. Are there courses or resources that you could access to learn specific techniques in this area?

_____

_____

_____

G. What will be your first step?

_____

_____

_____

AREA 2

A. Identify an area of your self-concept that you'd like to change.

_____

_____

_____

B. Who would be a role model in this area – someone you could learn from through direct observation?

_____

_____

_____

C. What abilities or qualities that you would like to acquire does the model possess in this area?

_____

_____

_____

D. What would be a reasonable amount of improvement to achieve in the area you picked?

_____

_____

_____

E. Who would be a person you can trust to seek balanced feedback from?

_____

_____

_____

F. Are there courses or resources that you could access to learn specific techniques in this area?

_____

_____

_____

G. What will be your first step?

_____

_____

_____

NAME _____

2.6   YOUR PUBLIC AND PRIVATE SELVES

◆ Activity Type: Invitation to Insight

PURPOSE
To help you explore your own experiences with your public and private selves.

INSTRUCTIONS
Complete the following questions.

1. Describe a significant experience, from any time in your life, in which you felt that you put on a **public face**.

_____

_____

_____

_____

_____

_____

2. How did your public self differ from your private self in this situation?

_____

_____

_____

_____

_____

_____

3. Explain how any of the following related to your reasons for using this public image.

Self-esteem _____

_____

_____

_____

Myth of perfection _____

_____

_____

_____

Reflected appraisal and distorted feedback _____

_____

_____

_____

Obsolete information _____

_____

_____

_____

Social expectations _____

_____

_____

_____

Social comparison _____

_____

_____

_____

4. How does your public/private self operate now in the area(s) you mentioned
   above? Has there been any change? What influences helped bring about the
   change?

_____

_____

_____

_____

_____

_____

_____

_____

_____

_____

_____

NAME _____

2.7   WHAT'S IN AN OBJECT?

◆❖ Activity Type: Invitation to Insight

PURPOSE
To examine the connection between the objects we value and our identity.

INSTRUCTIONS
1. Pick an object of yours that you value a great deal. This can be anything from a piece of jewellery that's been handed down to you, to a special photograph, to something you've made or been awarded. Anything that you would be very sad to lose will work.
2. Come together with a small group of classmates or friends who have each chosen an object too. If possible, each person should bring the item along when you meet. Take turns showing or describing the item you have chosen, explaining why it has such value to you.
3. In preparation for the meeting, try to answer the following question. If you have trouble answering it, though, you can ask the other group members for their thoughts.

What does it say about my personality or nature that I value this particular item so much?

_____

_____

_____

_____

_____

_____

_____

_____

_____

_____

_____

_____

_____

NAME _____

2.8   MEDIATED MESSAGES—IDENTITY MANAGEMENT

◆ Activity Type: Group Discussion

PURPOSE
To analyze your presentation of self in mediated communication.

INSTRUCTION
Discuss each of the questions below in your group. Prepare written answers for your instructor, or be prepared to contribute to a large group discussion, comparing your experiences with those of others in your class.

1. Describe ways in which messages from the mass media (e.g., radio, television, film, magazines, newspapers, books) have shaped your self-concept and the self-concepts of people you know well.

    _____

    _____

    _____

2. To the degree that messages from the mass media have a detrimental effect on your self-concept (or that of others), what can you do to overcome their detrimental effect?

    _____

    _____

    _____

3. Identity management is important in mediated contexts, as well as in face-to-face communication. Describe how you manage identity in the mediated contexts you most commonly use.

    _____

    _____

    _____

4. Your textbook states that people often prefer mediated channels when their own self-presentation is threatened. Give examples to support this claim here.

    _____

    _____

    _____

STUDY GUIDE

CROSSWORD PUZZLE

Across

1 the identity type that refers to a self-concept that is strongly "I" oriented, common in cultures where the main desire is to promote the self

8 the socially approved identity that a communicator tries to present

9 the tendency to look for people who confirm our self-concept

Down

1 the image one presents to others

2 the process of attending to one's behaviour and using these observations to shape the way one behaves

3 the identity that refers to a self-concept that is highly dependent on belonging to a group, common in cultures where the main desire is to build connections between the self and others

4 information that was once true about the self but is no longer true

5 a prophecy that is a prediction or expectation of an event that makes the outcome more likely to occur than would otherwise have been the case

6 the type of goal we have when we put on a public image as a way to command respect

7 the self that refers to the person we believe ourselves to be in moments of candour

9 _____ comparison: evaluation of oneself in terms of or by comparison with others

MATCHING

Match the terms in column 1 with their definitions in column 2.

_____ 1. cognitive conservatism

_____ 2. ideal self

_____ 3. identity management

_____ 4. perceived self

_____ 5. presenting self

_____ 6. reference groups

_____ 7. reflected appraisal

_____ 8. self-concept

_____ 9. self-fulfilling prophecy

_____ 10. significant other

_____ 11. social comparison

_____ 12. collective identity

_____ 13. individualistic identity

_____ 14. self-verification

_____ 15. self-monitoring

_____ 16. obsolete information

a. the relatively stable set of perceptions that each individual holds of himself or herself

b. a prediction or expectation of an event that makes the outcome more likely to occure than would otherwise have been the case

c. the process of observing one's behaviour and using these observations to shape the way one behaves

d. the image a person presents to others

e. the person each wishes to be

f. the theory that a person's self-concept matches the way that the person believes others regard him or her

g. a self-concept that is highly dependent on belonging to a group, common in cultures where the main desire is to build connections between the self and others

h. the communication strategies that people use to influence how others view them

i. groups against which we compare ourselves, thereby influencing our self-concept and self-esteem

j. a person whose opinion is important enough to affect one's self-concept strongly

k. the tendency to seek and attend to information that conforms to an exising self-concept

l. the person whom we believe ourselves to be in moments of candour

m. evaluation of oneself in terms of or by comparison with others

n. a self-concept that is strongly "I" oriented, common in cultures where the main desire is to promote the self

o. the tendency to look for people who confirm our self-concept

p. past successes or failures that no longer hold true for the self

TRUE/FALSE

Mark the statements below as true or false. Correct statements that are false on the lines below to create a true statement.

_____   **1.** Fortunately, unintentional messages do not affect our self-concept.

_____

_____   **2.** We shouldn't acknowledge the things we excel at because we will develop an overly positive self-concept.

_____

_____   **3.** The influence of significant others becomes less powerful as we grow older.

_____

_____   **4.** People who dislike themselves are likely to believe that others won't like them either.

_____

_____   **5.** Research has shown that people with high self-esteem seek out partners who view them unfavourably because they are strong enough to take the criticism.

_____

_____   **6.** Luckily, your self-concept is not affected by the language that you speak.

_____

_____   **7.** In individualistic societies, there is a higher degree of communication apprehension.

_____

_____   **8.** The self-concept is such a powerful force on the personality that it not only determines how you see yourself in the present but also can actually influence your future behaviour and that of others.

_____

_____   **9.** Research shows that people who believe they are incompetent are more likely than others to pursue rewarding relationships in an attempt to ally themselves with competent people.

_____

_____   **10.** The communication strategies we use to influence how others view us are all conscious behaviours.

_____

COMPLETION

Fill in the blanks below with the correct terms chosen from the list below.

distorted feedback obsolete information self-delusion
cognitive conservatism ego buster   realistic expectations
realistic perceptions manner   setting
appearance

1. _____ describes the inclination of our self-concept to remain the same even when we get feedback about ourself that is inconsistent with that self-concept.

2. _____ is someone who acts to reduce your self-esteem.

3. _____ are messages that others send to you that are unrealistically positive or negative.

4. _____ consists of a communicator's words and nonverbal actions that help create a front.

5. _____ refers to something that was once true but no longer is, although it might still be the basis of a current perception.

6. _____ refers to the personal items people use to shape an image.

7. _____ is the inability to see a real need for change in the self due to holding an unrealistically favourable picture of yourself.

8. _____ are reasonable goals to set for self-growth.

9. _____ refers to the physical items we use to influence how others view us.

10. _____ are relatively accurate views of the strengths and weaknesses of the self.

MULTIPLE CHOICE

Identify which principle influences the self-concept in each example. Place the letter of the correct term on the line adjacent to each description.
 a. obsolete information
 b. distorted feedback
 c. emphasis on perfection
 d. social expectations

_____ 1. You did a great job as a cashier last year and can't understand why your boss at your new sales job isn't equally impressed.

_____ 2. You just received a test mark of 98 out of 100. You spend the rest of the day upset that you lost those 2 marks.

_____ **3.** You were at a party and someone complimented you on your great taste in clothes. You felt uncomfortable and instead started talking about how great the party was.

_____ **4.** Your best friend agrees with you that the teachers are really marking your work unfairly (even though she privately thinks your work isn't very good).

_____ **5.** Ling says that you are insensitive to her perspective despite your many attempts to listen honestly to her and to empathize with her.

_____ **6.** You pay a lot of attention to the magazines showing perfectly dressed and groomed individuals and keep wishing you could look as good as they do.

_____ **7.** You think of yourself as the shy fifth grader despite being at the social hub of at least three clubs on campus.

_____ **8.** You feel uncomfortable accepting the compliments your friends honestly give you.

_____ **9.** You're exhausted by trying to get all A's, work 30 hours a week, and be a loving romantic partner at the same time. You don't see how so many other people manage to get it all done.

_____ **10.** You have been really trying harder to get your assignments in on time and have been very successful. You handed the last one in late, though, because of illness. Your instructor remarked that "you haven't changed – you're still the old irresponsible you."

Choose the *best* answer for each statement below:

11. Deciding which face – which part of you – to reveal is termed
   a. frontwork.
   b. identity management.
   c. hypocrisy.
   d. two-faced syndrome.

12. The most significant part of a person's self-concept
   a. is the social roles the person plays.
   b. is his or her appearance.
   c. is his or her accomplishments.
   d. will vary from person to person.

13. The self-concept begins
   a. at conception.
   b. in the womb.
   c. during the first year of life.
   d. at the onset of puberty.

14. Which of the following could be an example of a self-fulfilling prophecy?

   a. Sid is born with a very large nose.
   b. Marguerita has a very large, extended family.
   c. Serge is a Russian immigrant.
   d. Joy has given up on trying to talk to her unreasonable father.

15. The fact that none of us can see ourselves completely accurately illustrates the
_____ nature of the self-concept.

   a. subjective
   b. objective
   c. unrealistic
   d. verification

STUDY GUIDE ANSWERS

CROSSWORD PUZZLE

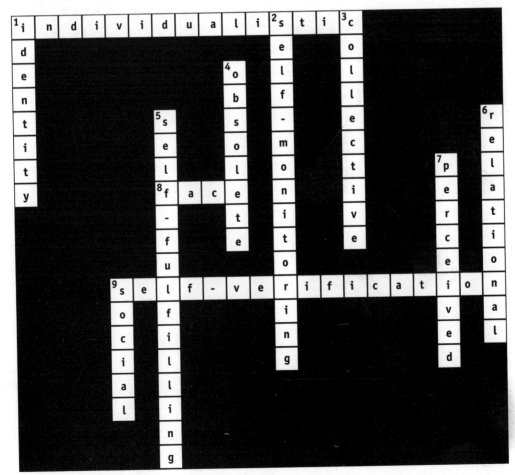

MATCHING

1. k	**5.** d	**9.** b	**13.** n
2. e	**6.** i	**10.** j	**14.** o
3. h	**7.** f	**11.** m	**15.** c
4. l	**8.** a	**12.** g	**16.** p

TRUE/FALSE

1. F	**5.** F	**9.** F
2. F	**6.** F	**10.** F
3. T	**7.** F	
4. T	**8.** T	

COMPLETION

1. cognitive conservatism	**5.** obsolete information	**9.** setting
2. ego buster	**6.** appearance	**10.** realistic perceptions
3. distorted feedback	**7.** self-delusion	
4. manner	**8.** realistic expectations	

MULTIPLE CHOICE

1. a	**4.** b	**7.** a	**10.** b	**13.** c
2. c	**5.** b	**8.** d	**11.** b ,	**14.** d
3. d	**6.** c	**9.** c	**12.** d	**15.** a

CHAPTER 3

Perception: What You See Is What You Get

OUTLINE

Use this outline to take notes as you read the chapter in the text and/or as your instructor lectures in class.

I. **The perception process**

   A. **Selection**
      1. Factors that influence selection
         a. Intense stimuli
         b. Repetitious stimuli
         c. Contrast or change in stimulation
         d. Motives
      2. Distortions in selection

   B. **Organization**
      1. Figure–ground organization
      2. Perceptual schema
         a. Physical constructs
         b. Role constructs
         c. Interaction constructs
         d. Psychological constructs
         e. Membership constructs
      3. Effects of organization
         a. Forms impressions of others
         b. Affects the way we relate to others
         c. May lead to inaccurate generalizations
            1) Stereotyping
            2) Punctuation

   C. **Interpretation**
      1. Relational satisfaction
      2. Degree of involvement with the other person

3. Past experience
4. Assumptions about human behaviour
5. Expectations
6. Knowledge
7. Self-concept

II.   Influences on perception

A. Physiological
1. Senses
2. Age
3. Health
4. Fatigue
5. Hunger
6. Biological cycles

B. Cultural Differences
1. Language translations
2. Value of talk
3. Nonverbal behaviours
4. Ethnicity
5. Geography

C. Social Roles

D. Gender Roles

E. Occupational Roles

F. Self-Concept
1. Judgments of others
2. Judgments of self

G. Shared Narratives

III.   The accuracy—and inaccuracy—of perception

A. We Often Judge Ourselves More Charitably than Others

B. We Tend to Favour Negative Impressions of Others over Positive Ones

C. We Are Influenced by What Is Most Obvious

D. We Cling to First Impressions

E. We Tend to Assume Others Are Similar to Us

IV.   Perception checking to prevent misunderstandings

A. Elements of Perception Checking
1. Describe behaviour
2. Interpret behaviour two ways
3. Request clarification

    B. **Perception-Checking Considerations**
        1. Completeness
        2. Nonverbal congruency
        3. Cultural rules
            a. Low-context cultures
            b. High-context cultures

V. Empathy and communication

    A. **Empathy Defined**
        1. Empathy – ability to re-create another's perspective
            a. Perspective taking
            b. Emotional dimension
            c. Genuine concern
        2. Sympathy – compassion for another's predicament

    B. **The "Pillow Method"—A Tool for Building Empathy**
        1. Position 1: I'm right, you're wrong
        2. Position 2: You're right, I'm wrong
        3. Position 3: Both right, both wrong
        4. Position 4: The issue isn't as important as it seems
        5. Conclusion: There is truth in all four perspectives

KEY TERMS

Use these key terms to review major concepts from your text. Write the definition for each key term in the space to the right.

androgynous _____

attribution _____

cultural differences _____

empathy _____

figure–ground organization _____

gender roles _____

high-context culture _____

interaction constructs _____

interpretation _____

low-context culture _____

membership constructs _____

narrative _____

occupational roles _____

organization _____

perception _____

perception checking _____

perceptual schema _____

physical constructs _____

physiological influences _____

pillow method _____

psychological constructs _____

punctuation _____

role constructs _____

selection _____

self-serving bias _____

social roles _____

stereotyping _____

subcultural differences _____

sympathy _____

NAME _____

ACTIVITIES

3.1   FROM STEREOTYPES TO EMPATHY

◆ Activity Type: Invitation to Insight

PURPOSE
To brainstorm ways to build empathy based on your own experiences with stereotyping.

INSTRUCTIONS
Answer the following questions.

1. Are there any groups that you have had or still do have a large or small stereotype about? Try to answer this question as candidly as possible. If you honestly can't think of any groups, you can pick someone you know well who seems to believe in a stereotype. Below, identify the group that the stereotype is about. (Pick one group only.)

    _____

2. What was(were) or is(are) the stereotype(s)? (For example, you might begin: People in this group are . . .)

    _____

    _____

3. What do you think were or are the sources for the stereotype(s)? (For example, the sources might be one or two bad experiences, advertising, news stories, etc.)

    _____

    _____

    _____

4. If you have already gotten past the stereotype(s) you have described, explain what happened to change your perception of members of that group. If you still hold to the stereotypic view, what are some ways in which you could challenge yourself to see if the view is a stereotype or, in fact, an accurate generalization?

    _____

    _____

    _____

NAME _____

3.2   EXPLORING THE FUTURE

◆ Activity Type: Invitation to Insight

PURPOSE
To better understand current perceptions about upcoming events.

INSTRUCTIONS
1. Identify three upcoming events (e.g., a trip to the dentist).
2. For each event, describe your general perception – is it more of a good thing that it will be happening, or more of a bad thing?
3. Analyze your general perception by trying to apply each of the following factors found in Chapter 3 of *Looking Out/Looking In*:
   a. your degree of involvement with the people involved
   b. your past experiences
   c. your assumptions about human behaviour
   d. your expectations
   e. relevant knowledge that you have or don't have
   f. your self-concept
   g. relational satisfaction

EVENT 1
A.   Your general perception of the event _____

B.   Analysis of your general perception using the factors identified in the instructions

_____

_____

_____

_____

_____

_____

_____

_____

_____

_____

EVENT 2

A.   Your general perception of the event _____

B.   Analysis of your general perception using the factors identified in the instructions

_____

_____

_____

_____

_____

_____

_____

_____

_____

_____

_____

_____

EVENT 3

A.   Your general perception of the event _____

B.   Analysis of your general perception using the factors identified in the instructions

_____

_____

_____

_____

_____

_____

_____

_____

_____

_____

_____

_____

_____

NAME _____

3.3   SHIFTING PERSPECTIVES (PILLOW METHOD)

◆ Activity Type: Invitation to Insight

PURPOSES
1. To help you understand how others view an interpersonal issue.
2. To help you recognize the merits and drawbacks of each person's perspective.
3. To help you recognize how an interpersonal issue may not be as important as it first seems.

INSTRUCTIONS
1. Select one disagreement or other issue that is now affecting an interpersonal relationship.
2. Record enough background information for an outsider to understand the issue. Who is involved? How long has the disagreement been going on? What are the basic issues involved?
3. Describe the issue from each of the four positions listed below.
4. Record your conclusions at the end of this exercise.

Background Information

_____

_____

_____

_____

Position 1: Explain how you are right and the other person is wrong.

_____

_____

_____

_____

_____

Position 2: Explain how the other person's position is correct, or at least understandable.

_____

_____

_____

_____

_____

Position 3: Show that there are both correct (or understandable) and mistaken (or unreasonable) parts of both positions.

_____

_____

_____

_____

_____

Position 4: Describe at least two ways in which the elements developed in positions 1–3 might affect your relationship. Describe at least one way in which the issue might be seen as _less_ important than it was originally and describe at least one way in which the issue might be seen as _more_ important than it was originally.

_____

_____

_____

_____

_____

CONCLUSION

Explain how there is some truth in each of the preceding positions. Also explain how viewing the issue from each of the preceding positions has changed your perception of the issue and how it may change your behaviour in the future. Explain how this issue and your understanding of it affect your relationship.

_____

_____

_____

_____

_____

NAME _____

3.4   OBSERVATION AND PERCEPTION

❖ Activity Type: Skill Builder

PURPOSES
1. To report your observations of another person clearly and accurately.
2. To report at least two interpretations about the meaning of your observations to another person.
3. To discuss and evaluate the various choices you have available to you when dealing with perceptual problems.

INSTRUCTIONS
1. As a group, detail three situations below in which there are potential perceptual problems.
2. Use the form below to record behaviour for each relationship listed.
3. For each example of behaviour, record two plausible interpretations.
4. Record a request for feedback.
5. With others in the group, rehearse how you could share with the person in question each example of behaviour and the possible interpretations you have developed.
6. Evaluate the various other options you have to check out perceptions. Describe the probable outcome of each.

EXAMPLE
Perceptual problem *Jill's math professor is really annoying her – calling on her for answers and trying to get her involved more in the class. Jill is uncomfortable about this, but she is afraid that the professor might pay even more attention to her if she brings it up.*
Perception-checking statement *Professor Smith, I'm confused about something.*

Behaviour *I've noticed that you call on me quite often – at least once each class, whether or not I raise my hand.*
Interpretation A *Sometimes I wonder if you're trying to catch me unprepared.*
Interpretation B *On the other hand, sometimes I think you're trying to challenge me by forcing me to keep on my toes.*
Request for feedback *Can you tell me why you call on me so often?*

Perception-checking options

1. *Jill could do nothing. Perhaps it would be better to wait and see if she has been imagining this by watching a bit more.*
2. *Jill could start initiating answers herself and see if Professor Smith changes her behaviour.*
3. *Jill could just tell the prof that she doesn't like being called on. This might alienate her in the prof's eyes, however, and might affect her grade.*

4.   Jill could just ask if the prof was trying to embarrass her. We thought the prof might not know what Jill was referring to, though, if she didn't describe the behaviour. The prof probably teaches hundreds of students and might not realize what's going on from Jill's perspective.

5.   Jill could do the complete perception-checking statement we wrote above. Our group thought this has a good chance for success if the prof didn't get defensive. If Jill could deliver the statement in a nondefensive tone and then follow it up with how much she likes the class, perhaps the prof would realize how much Jill is bothered.

SITUATION 1

Perceptual problem _____

_____

_____

Perception-checking statement _____

   Behaviour _____

   Interpretation A _____

   Interpretation B _____

   Request for feedback _____

Perception-checking options

_____

_____

_____

_____

_____

SITUATION 2

Perceptual problem _____

_____

_____

Perception-checking statement _____

   Behaviour _____

   Interpretation A _____

   Interpretation B _____

   Request for feedback _____

Perception-checking options

_____

_____

_____

_____

_____

SITUATION 3

Perceptual problem _____

_____

_____

Perception-checking statement _____

Behaviour _____

Interpretation A _____

Interpretation B _____

Request for feedback _____

Perception-checking options

_____

_____

_____

_____

_____

3.5 APPLYING PERCEPTION CHECKING

◆❖ Activity Type: Skill Builder

PURPOSE
To prepare, deliver, and evaluate effective perception-checking statements.

INSTRUCTIONS
1. Choose two people with whom you have relational concerns. Give careful consideration to the partners you choose, choose concerns that are real and important, and allow yourself enough time to discuss your concerns with each partner.
2. Identify the concern, its importance to you, and consider the best time and place to approach each person.
3. Prepare perception-checking statements to deliver to each person.
4. Deliver your perception statements, discussing with each person your understanding of his or her behaviour and the accuracy or inaccuracy of your perceptions. Or discuss why you decided not to use perception checking in this situation – and what you did alternatively.

PARTNER 1

Part One: Describing Your Concern

Partner's name_____

A. Describe your primary concern _____

_____

_____

B. Why is it important to you to clarify this matter?_____

_____

_____

C. When and where is the best time to talk with this person? _____

_____

_____

Part Two: Preparing Your Perception-Checking Statement

A.   Describe your observations of the other person's behaviour. _____

_____

_____

B.   Write one interpretation that you believe could explain the behaviours you have observed.

_____

_____

_____

C.   Now write a second interpretation that is distinctly different from your previous one and that you believe could also explain the behaviour you have observed.

_____

_____

_____

D.   Make a request for feedback._____

Part Three: Sharing Your Perception-Checking Statement

Meet with your partner and (1) share your description of this person's behaviour, (2) explain both of your interpretations of the behaviour, and (3) ask your partner to react to the interpretations you have shared.

Describe the outcome of your conversation with your partner._____

_____

_____

Or, if you think perception checking would not be appropriate or effective, explain why you decided not to use perception checking in this situation – and what you did instead.

_____

_____

_____

PARTNER 2

Part One: Describing Your Concern

Partner's name_____

A. Describe your primary concern._____

_____

_____

B. Why is it important to you to clarify this matter?_____

_____

_____

C. When and where is the best time to talk with this person? _____

_____

_____

Part Two: Preparing Your Perception-Checking Statement

A. Describe your observations of the other person's behaviour. _____

_____

_____

B. Write one interpretation that you believe could explain the behaviours you have
observed.

_____

_____

_____

C. Now write a second interpretation that is distinctly different from your previous
one and that you believe could also explain the behaviour you have observed.

_____

_____

_____

D. Make a request for feedback._____

Part Three: Sharing Your Perception-Checking Statement

Meet with your partner and (1) share your description of this person's behaviour, (2) explain both of your interpretations of the behaviour, and (3) ask your partner to react to the interpretations you have shared.

Describe the outcome of your conversation with your partner. _____

_____

_____

_____

Or, if you think perception checking would not be appropriate or effective, explain why you decided not to use perception checking in this situation – and what you did instead.

_____

_____

_____

SUMMARY

1. How accurate were your interpretations in the two situations above?

    _____

    _____

    _____

2. Based on your experiences in this exercise, in what circumstances are your interpretations accurate? When are they likely to be inaccurate? Consider the people involved, the topic of communication, and your personal moods and thoughts.

    _____

    _____

    _____

3. How did your partners react when you communicated by using perception checking? How did these reactions differ from the reactions you get when you jump to conclusions instead of using perception checking? If you decided not to use perception checking, what did you do instead and what were the results? How could this improve your relationships in the future?

_____

_____

_____

_____

4. Based on your experience in this exercise, when and how can you use perception checking in your everyday communication? With whom? In what situations? What difference will using perception checking make in your interpersonal relationships?

_____

_____

_____

_____

NAME _____

3.6   PERCEPTION-CHECKING PRACTICE

◆❖ Activity Type: Skill Builder

PURPOSE
To create effective perception-checking statements.

INSTRUCTIONS

OPTION A:
Practice writing perception-checking statements for items 1–12 below.

OPTION B:
1. Join with a partner to create a dyad. Label one person A and the other B.
2. Both A and B should write perception-checking statements for items 1–12 below.
3. A then delivers items 1–6 orally to B. B should use the checklist from Activity 3.7 to rate A's responses for these items.
4. B delivers items 7–12 orally to A. A should now use the checklist to rate B's responses for these items.

OPTION C:

Practise items 1–12 below orally with a partner. Deliver your best perception check in class while your instructor evaluates you.

EXAMPLE

Yesterday you saw your friend walking on the beach engaged in what looked to you like an intense conversation with your recent date, Chris.

Perception-checking statement *When I saw you yesterday walking on the beach with Chris, I didn't know what to make of it. I thought you might be talking about that class you're taking together, but I also wondered whether you're interested in dating Chris. Are you interested in Chris as a friend, or as a date?*

1. During last week's exam you thought you saw your friend Jim, who sits next to you in class, looking at your paper.

_____

_____

_____

2. Ever since the school year began, members of your family have made a point of asking how you are doing several times each month. They have just asked again.

_____

_____

_____

3. Your friend Kwok was driving you home from a party last night when he began to weave the car between lanes on the highway. You were uncomfortable, but didn't say anything then. Now it is the next morning and Kwok shows up to take you to a class. You have decided to bring up the incident.

_____

_____

_____

4. It seems that every time you've left your house recently, your roommate has run after you, asking for a ride somewhere. Your roommate has a car, but you haven't seen it lately. You are in a hurry now, and your roommate has just asked for another ride.

_____

_____

_____

5. You return home at night to find your roommate, Saied, reading on the couch. When you walk into the room and greet Saied, he grunts and turns his face away from you and keeps reading.

_____

_____

_____

6. Last week your instructor, Dr. Desroches, returned your exam with a low grade and the comment, "This kind of work paints a bleak picture for the future." You have approached him to discuss the remark.

_____

_____

_____

7. In one of your regular long-distance phone conversations you ask your favourite cousin, Mike, about the state of his up-and-down romantic life. He sighs and says, "Oh, it's OK, I guess."

_____

_____

_____

8. Your girlfriend or boyfriend (or spouse) announces that she or he plans to spend next Friday night with friends from work. You usually spend Friday nights alone together.

_____

_____

_____

9. Last week your supervisor at work, Ms. Freitas, gave you a big assignment. Three times since then she has asked you whether you're having any trouble with it.

_____

_____

_____

10. Last weekend your next-door neighbour, Steve, raked a big pile of leaves near your property line, promising to clean them up after work on Monday. It's Wednesday, and the wind is blowing the leaves into your yard.

_____

_____

_____

11. One of your classmates sits by you every day in class and runs after you to walk across campus; now he has started calling you at home every evening. He now suggests that you do some things on the weekend together.

_____

_____

_____

12. You've noticed one of your colleagues looking over at you a number of times during the past few days. At first she looked away quickly, but now she smiles every time you look up and catch her looking at you. You've been under a lot of pressure at work lately and have been extremely busy. You can't understand why she keeps looking at you. You've decided to ask.

_____

_____

_____

NAME _____

3.7   PERCEPTION CHECKING

❖ Activity Type: Oral Skill

PURPOSE
To evaluate your skill at using perception-checking statements.

INSTRUCTIONS
1. Identify a situation in your life in which a perception check might be appropriate. Describe the situation to the person who will be evaluating your skill check.
2. Deliver a complete perception check to your evaluator, without using notes, following the criteria listed in Chapter 3 of *Looking Out/Looking In* and outlined in the checklist on the following page.
3. Then describe below
   a. how well perception checking might (or might not) work in the situation you have chosen. If you do not think a complete perception check is the best approach for this situation, explain why and describe a more promising alternative.
   b. the degree to which you could (or could not) increase your communicative competence by using perception checks in other situations.

How well might perception checking work in this situation?

_____

_____

_____

_____

_____

How could you increase your competence by using perception checking in other situations?

_____

_____

_____

_____

_____

CHECKLIST

_____　　　Describes background for potential perception-checking situation.

_____　　　Delivers complete perception check.

　　　　　　　_____　　　Reports at least one behaviour that describes what the person has said or done.

　　　　　　　_____　　　States two interpretations that are distinctly different, equally probable, and based on the reported behaviour.

　　　　　　　_____　　　Makes a sincere request for feedback clarifying how to interpret the reported behaviour.

_____　　　Verbal and nonverbal behaviour.

　　　　　　　_____　　　Reflects sincere desire for clarification of the perception.

　　　　　　　_____　　　Sounds realistic and consistent with style of the speaker.

　　　　　　　_____　　　Uses nonthreatening, nondefensive voice and eye contact.

_____　　　Realistically and clearly assesses how perception checking and other alternatives can be used in everyday life.

　　　　　　　_____　　　In situation described here.

　　　　　　　_____　　　In other situations (be specific).

NAME_____

3.8   YOUR CALL—PERCEPTION

◆❖ Activity Type: Group Discussion

PURPOSES

1. To help you reflect upon and judge a communication transaction in terms of the perceptions of the persons involved.
2. To help you use perception checking to clarify a situation.
3. To help you explain perceptual factors that may contribute to misunderstandings.

INSTRUCTIONS

Use the case below and the discussion questions that follow to explore the variety of communication issues involved in communication and perception. Make notes on this page, add other pages on your own, or prepare a group report/analysis based on your discussion. Add your own experiences to individualize the analysis to make it "Your Call."

CASE

Jorge is a registered nurse at a facility that cares for about 80 elderly patients. Jorge has been at the facility longer than any of the other nurses and usually has his choice of schedule; he believes he deserves his choice because of his service and seniority. In the last year, there has been a shortage of nurses. Jorge's supervisor, Marisa, has been trying to hire new nurses, some of whom will work only if they can have Jorge's schedule. Marisa and Jorge are meeting to discuss the situation.

1. What factors are likely to influence the perceptions of Jorge and Marisa?

   _____

   _____

2. Prepare perception-checking statements for both Jorge and Marisa to deliver to one another.

   _____

   _____

3. What misperceptions may be in operation in this situation? (Any punctuation?)

   _____

   _____

4. How can Marisa and Jorge communicate competently in order to come to a constructive conclusion to this situation?

   _____

   _____

STUDY GUIDE

CROSSWORD PUZZLE

Across

1 a method that examines the four sides and middle of a perceptual issue

2 the degree of empathy you would have if you were able to appreciate the factors behind a friend's desperate actions, even though you are not at all in favour of what he or she did

6 the ability to project oneself into another person's point of view so as to experience the other's thoughts and feelings

8 constructs that are perceptual schema that categorize people according to the groups to which they belong

12 possessing both masculine and feminine traits

14 the type of roles that cause perceptual problems by creating rigidly defined expectations based on gender and occupation

Down

1 constructs that are perceptual schema that categorize people according to their appearances

3 perceptions are strongly influenced by these roles based on sex-typed behaviours

4 constructs that are perceptual schema that categorize people according to their social behaviours

5 compassion for another's situation

7 the process of attaching meaning to behaviour

9 this type of perceptual influence is created by our body's design and condition

10 exaggerated generalizations associated with a categorizing system

11 constructs that are perceptual schema that categorize people according to their apparent personalities

13 constructs that are perceptual schema that categorize people according to their social positions

COMPLETION

Fill in the blanks below with the correct terms chosen from the list below.

membership constructs   physical constructs   sympathy
interaction constructs   perceptual schema   shared narrative
psychological constructs   role constructs   stereotypes
attribution

1. _____ are the cognitive frameworks that allow individuals to organize perceptual data that they have selected from the environment.

There are five different ways that we organize these frameworks:

2. _____ are perceptual schema that categorize people according to their social position.

3. _____ are perceptual schema that categorize people according to their appearance.

4. _____ are perceptual schema that categorize people according to their apparent personalities.

5. _____ are perceptual schema that categorize people according to their social behaviour.

6. _____ are perceptual schema that categorize people according to the groups to which they belong.

7. _____ is the process by which people make sense of an event through the trading of interpretations about the event.

8. _____ is feeling compassion for another person's predicament.

9. _____ are exaggerated beliefs associated with a categorizing system.

10. _____ is the process of interpreting, or attaching meaning to, another person's behaviour.

MULTIPLE CHOICE

For each of the following statements, identify which element of the perception-checking statement is missing. Place the letter of the most accurate evaluation of the statement on the line before the statement.

   a.   This statement doesn't describe behaviour.
   b.   This statement doesn't give two distinctly different interpretations.
   c.   This statement neglects to request clarification of the perception.
   d.   There is nothing missing from this perception-checking statement.

_____   **1.**   "When you didn't return any of my phone calls, I thought you were avoiding me, or maybe it was some other reason. Why didn't you call back?"

_____   **2.**   "When you went straight to bed when you came home, I thought you were sick. Are you all right?"

_____   **3.**   "You must be either really excited about your grades or anxious to talk about something important. What's going on?"

_____   **4.**   "When you ran out smiling, I figured you were glad to see me and ready to go, or maybe you were having such a good time here you wanted to stay longer."

_____   **5.**   "When you didn't do our grocery shopping today like you usually do on Mondays, I figured you weren't feeling good or you were still mad at me from yesterday."

_____   **6.**   "When you told me you expected to get an outline with my report, I thought you were trying to trick me into doing more work, or maybe you didn't realize that wasn't part of my job."

_____   **7.**   "When you told everyone my parents own the company, you must have been indicating I was hired here only because of them. Is that what you think?"

_____   **8.**   "When you gave me an F on that last assignment, I thought it was because you have something against me . . . Am I right?"

_____   **9.**   "Why is it that you're so pleased with yourself? Did you win the lottery or accomplish something great? What's up?"

_____   **10.**   "Dad, when you told my friend Art what a great athlete you think I am, I thought you were either really proud of me and wanted to brag a little, or maybe you wanted to see what Art and I had in common by the way he responded. What were you up to?"

STUDY GUIDE ANSWERS

CROSSWORD PUZZLE

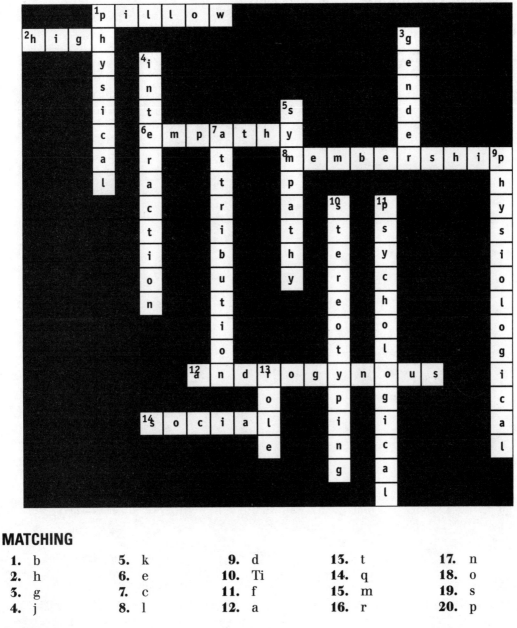

MATCHING

1. b	**5.** k	**9.** d	**13.** t	**17.** n
2. h	**6.** e	**10.** Ti	**14.** q	**18.** o
3. g	**7.** c	**11.** f	**15.** m	**19.** s
4. j	**8.** l	**12.** a	**16.** r	**20.** p

TRUE/FALSE

1. F	**3.** F	**5.** F	**7.** F	**9.** F
2. T	**4.** T	**6.** T	**8.** F	**10.** F

COMPLETION

1. perceptual schema
2. role constructs
3. physical constructs
4. psychological constructs
5. interaction constructs
6. membership constructs
7. shared narrative
8. sympathy
9. stereotypes
10. attribution

MULTIPLE CHOICE

1. b
2. b
3. a
4. c
5. c
6. c
7. b
8. b
9. a
10. d

CHAPTER 4

Emotions: Thinking, Feeling, and Acting

OUTLINE

Use this outline to take notes as you read the chapter in the text and/or as your instructor lectures in class.

I.   What are emotions?

    A.   Physiological Changes

    B.   Nonverbal Reactions

    C.   Verbal Expression

    D.   Cognitive Interpretations

II.   Types of emotions

    A.   Primary and Mixed

    B.   Intense and Mild

III.   Influences on emotional expression

    A.   Culture

    B.   Gender

    C.   Social Conventions

    D.   Social Roles

    E.   Emotional Contagion

    F.   Fear of Self-Disclosure

IV.   Guidelines for expressing emotions

A.   **Think about How to Describe Feelings**
1.   Avoid emotional counterfeits
2.   Express verbally
   a.   Use single words
   b.   Describe what's happening to you
   c.   Describe what you'd like to do
   d.   Use metaphors
3.   Avoid discounting feelings
4.   Avoid coded feelings
5.   Focus on a specific set of circumstances

B.   **Share Multiple Feelings**

C.   **Recognize the Difference between Feeling, Talking, and Acting**

D.   **Accept Responsibility for Your Feelings**

E.   **Consider When and Where to Express Your Feelings**

V.   Managing difficult emotions

A.   **Facilitative and Debilitative Emotions**
1.   Intensity
2.   Duration

B.   **Thoughts Cause Feelings**

C.   **Irrational Thinking and Debilitative Emotions**
1.   Fallacy of perfection
2.   Fallacy of approval
3.   Fallacy of shoulds
4.   Fallacy of overgeneralization
   a.   Limited amount of evidence
   b.   Exaggerated shortcomings
   c.   Abuse of the verb "to be"
5.   Fallacy of causation
   a.   Belief that you cause emotions/pain for others
      1)   You fail to have your own needs met
      2)   You begin to resent others
      3)   Others can't trust you
   b.   Belief that others cause your emotions
6.   Fallacy of helplessness
7.   Fallacy of catastrophic expectations

D.   **Minimizing Debilitative Emotions**
1.   Monitor your emotional reactions
2.   Note the activating event
3.   Record your self-talk
4.   Dispute your irrational beliefs

KEY TERMS

Use these key terms to review major concepts from your text. Write the definition for each key term in the space to the right.

activating event _____

cognitive interpretations _____

debilitative emotions _____

duration _____

emotional contagion _____

emotional counterfeits _____

emotions _____

facilitative emotions _____

fallacy of approval _____

fallacy of catastrophic expectations _____

fallacy of causation _____

fallacy of helplessness _____

fallacy of overgeneralization _____

fallacy of perfection _____

fallacy of shoulds _____

intensity _____

irrational fallacies _____

metaphors _____

mixed emotions _____

nonverbal reactions _____

physiological changes _____

Plutchik's "emotion wheel" _____

primary emotions _____

proprioceptive stimuli _____

rational–emotive therapy _____

self-talk _____

NAME _____

ACTIVITIES

4.1   IDENTIFYING SPECIFIC AND MULTIPLE EMOTIONS

◆❖ Activity Type: Skill Builder

PURPOSES
1. To develop your ability to identify emotions in a more specific way.
2. To develop your ability to recognize multiple and mixed emotions.

INSTRUCTIONS
1. Read the story "An Emotional Tale" by Judith Rolls in Chapter 4 of *Looking Out/Looking In.*
2. Pick out and describe on the following form three different single "moments" or points in the story (e.g., when the doctor informed Heather that she had an ectopic pregnancy).
3. For each moment you selected, try to identify specific emotions being felt by one of the participants. When you do this, try to use emotion words that are specific or unique to the situation. For example, suppose that a friend says to you, "What a mooch! He sits around all day and helps himself to everything but never lends a hand in return. He's really starting to bug me!" You could say, in a general way, that your friend is feeling "angry," "frustrated," "irritated," etc. But if you examine the specific situation, you might come up with words such as "used," "abused," "powerless," or "resentful."
4. For the participant you selected in each moment, determine if there were multiple feelings, and if so, were they related to each other or seemingly unrelated or "mixed."
5. Conclude the activity by comparing notes with other classmates. Did anyone come up with especially illustrative words or words that picked up emotions you missed?

MOMENT 1
A. Describe briefly the moment in the story (when and where it was, who was there, and what was happening).

_____

_____

_____

B. Identify one of the participants and as many specific emotions as possible that he or she was feeling. Give reasons why you think he or she was feeling that way.

Person _____

Emotion(s) _____

Reason _____

_____

_____

C. If you identified more than one emotion above, were they mixed?

_____

_____

MOMENT 2

A. Describe briefly the moment in the story (when and where it was, who was there, and what was happening).

_____

_____

_____

B. Identify one of the participants and as many specific emotions as possible that he or she was feeling. Give reasons why you think he or she was feeling that way.

Person _____

Emotion(s) _____

Reason _____

_____

_____

C. If you identified more than one emotion above, were they mixed?

_____

_____

MOMENT 3

A. Describe briefly the moment in the story (when and where it was, who was there, and what was happening).

_____

_____

_____

B. Identify one of the participants and as many specific emotions as possible that he or she was feeling. Give reasons why you think he or she was feeling that way.

Person _____

Emotion(s) _____

Reason _____

_____

_____

C. If you identified more than one emotion above, were they mixed?

_____

_____

NAME _____

4.2   FIND THE FEELINGS

❖ Activity Type: Skill Builder

PURPOSES
1. To help you distinguish true feeling statements from counterfeit expressions of emotion.
2. To increase your ability to express your feelings clearly.

INSTRUCTIONS
1. In groups, identify the true feeling statements below.
2. Analyze the statements for accuracy of feeling (check your analysis at the end of this exercise).
3. Rewrite statements that do not clearly or accurately express the speaker's feelings. (HINT: Statements that could be prefaced with "I think" are not always expressions of emotions. If the statements could be preceded by "I am," there is a good likelihood that they express feelings.)
4. Record examples of your own at the end of the exercise.

EXAMPLE

That's the most disgusting thing I've ever heard!
Analysis *This isn't a satisfactory statement, since the speaker isn't clearly claiming that he or she is disgusted.*
Restatement *I'm upset and angry that those parents left their young children alone overnight.*

1. You're being awfully sensitive about that.

   Analysis _____

   _____

   Restatement _____

   _____

2. I can't figure out how to approach him.

   Analysis _____

   _____

Restatement _____

_____

3. I'm confused about what you want from me.

Analysis _____

_____

Restatement _____

_____

4. I feel as if you're trying to hurt me.

Analysis _____

_____

Restatement _____

_____

5. It's hopeless!

Analysis _____

_____

Restatement _____

_____

6. I don't know how to tell you this . . .

Analysis _____

_____

Restatement _____

_____

7. What's bothering you?

Analysis _____

_____

Restatement _____

_____

8. I feel like the rug's been pulled out from under me.

Analysis _____

_____

Restatement _____

_____

9. I feel like I've been stabbed in the back.

Analysis _____

_____

Restatement _____

_____

10. You're so pathetic.

Analysis _____

_____

Restatement _____

_____

Now record three feeling statements of your own. Analyze and, if necessary, restate.

11. _____

Analysis _____

_____

Restatement _____

_____

12. _____

Analysis _____

Restatement _____

_____

13. _____

Analysis _____

_____

Restatement _____

_____

ANSWERS TO ACTIVITY 4.2

1. The speaker here is labelling another's feelings, but saying nothing about his or her own. Is the speaker concerned, irritated, or indifferent to the other person's suspected sensitivity? We don't know. Possible restatement: "I'm worried that I teased you too much about your hair."
2. The emotion here is implied but not stated. The speaker might be frustrated, perplexed, or tired. Possible restatement: "I'm unsure about telling him the truth about my absence."
3. Here is a clear statement of the speaker's emotional state. Possible restate: "I'm confused about whether you want me to pay cash or charge it."
4. Just because we say "I feel" doesn't mean a feeling is being expressed. This is an interpretation statement. Possible restatement: "I'm anxious about trusting you after you lied to me last week."
5. How does the speaker feel about the hopeless situation: resigned, sad, desperate? We haven't been told. Possible restatement: "I feel frustrated after failing three math quizzes in a row."
6. Again, no feeling is stated. Is the speaker worried, afraid, distraught? Possible restatement: "I'm hesitant to tell you about my plans for the summer."
7. This could be a statement of concern, irritation, or genuine confusion. Nonverbal clues can help us decide, but a feeling statement would tell us for certain. Possible restatement: "I'm concerned that I may have offended you in some way."
8. Here's a metaphorical statement of feeling, strongly suggesting surprise or shock. This sort of message probably does an adequate job of expressing the emotion here, but it might be too vague for some people to understand. Possible restatement: "I feel insecure right now because I didn't get the job I was expecting."
9. This is another metaphorical statement of feeling, strongly suggesting hurt or betrayal. While this statement may do an adequate job of expressing the emotion, it might be misinterpreted by some people, and it might be too strong a statement for the actual situation. Possible restatement: "I'm hurt that Joe told you what I said in confidence."
10. This is the speaker's interpretation of someone else's behaviour. It contains no feeling. Possible restatement: "I'm irritated that you say you're tired and overworked when I've just worked a week of 10-hour shifts."

NAME _____

4.3   STATING EMOTIONS EFFECTIVELY

❖ Activity Type: Skill Builder

PURPOSE
To help you express clearly and appropriately the emotions you experience.

INSTRUCTIONS
1. Identify what's ineffective or unclear about each of the following feeling statements.
2. Rewrite the feeling statements, making them more effective. Use the following guidelines for sharing feelings:

> Recognize feelings
> Describe feelings (concise, not discounted, not coded, focused on specifics)
> Share multiple feelings
> Differentiate between feeling, talking, and acting
> Accept responsibility for your feelings
> Consider when and where to express

FEELING STATEMENT	IDENTIFY INEFFECTIVE, UNCLEAR ELEMENTS/REWRITE STATEMENT
EXAMPLE When you complimented me in front of everyone at the party, I was really embarrassed.	I didn't express the mixed emotions I was feeling. I could have expressed this better by saying "When you complimented me at the party, I was glad you were proud of me, but I was embarrassed that you did it in front of so many people."
1. You make me so mad.	
2. I can't believe you act like that – I don't want to see you anymore.	
3. I don't care if you are rushed. We have to settle this now.	

FEELING STATEMENT	IDENTIFY INEFFECTIVE, UNCLEAR ELEMENTS/REWRITE STATEMENT
4. I was a little ticked off when you didn't show up.	
5. You're always criticizing me.	
6. Sure would be nice if people expressed appreciation.	
7. You jerk – you forgot to put gas in the car.	
8. It's about time you paid up.	
9. You're the best! Thanks for everything.	
10. I feel like a heel.	
11. I guess I'm a little attracted to him.	
12. She sends me into outer space.	

NAME _____

4.4   EXPRESSING EMOTIONS APPROPRIATELY

◆ Activity Type: Skill Builder

PURPOSE
To expand your skill at expressing emotions appropriately.

INSTRUCTIONS
Identify and examine one of your own communication moments in which you felt dissatisfied. Then apply the theory in Chapter 5 of *Looking Out/Looking In* to possibly improve technique.

1. Describe a situation in which you wish you had expressed your emotions more appropriately.

   Describe the context. (What was happening at the time?)

   _____

   _____

   _____

   _____

   _____

   What were your feelings?

   _____

   _____

   _____

   _____

   How did you express your emotions at the time? (What did you say or do, or what didn't you say or do?)

   _____

   _____

   _____

   _____

   _____

Why was the way you expressed your emotions inappropriate or ineffective?

_____

_____

_____

_____

_____

_____

2. Did any of the influences on emotional expression described in Chapter 5 of the text (e.g., culture, gender, social conventions) affect your ability to express your emotions more appropriately in this situation? Which influences? Explain why you think this is the case.

_____

_____

_____

_____

_____

_____

_____

3. How would you change the way you verbally expressed your emotions to bring it in line with the guidelines for expressing emotions discussed in Chapter 5 of the text? What would you say differently, and why? Is there someone else to whom you should be communicating your emotions? If so, to whom? What would you say to this person? When? Where? Why? Etc. Be sure to refer to *specific* guidelines in your answer.

_____

_____

_____

_____

_____

_____

_____

_____

_____

_____

NAME _____

4.5   DISPUTING IRRATIONAL THOUGHTS

◆ Activity Type: Invitation to Insight

PURPOSE
To help you minimize debilitative emotions by eliminating irrational thinking.

INSTRUCTIONS
1. Use the chart on the following page to record incidents in which you experience communication-related debilitative emotions. The incidents needn't involve overwhelming feelings: mildly debilitative emotions are appropriate for consideration as well.
2. For each incident (activating event), record the self-talk that leads to the emotion you experienced.
3. If the self-talk you've identified is based on any of the irrational fallacies described in *Looking Out/Looking In*, identify them.
4. In each case where irrational thinking exists, dispute the irrational fallacies and provide an alternative, more rational interpretation of the event.
5. After completing the examples, record your conclusions here (or put them on a separate page).

CONCLUSIONS
1. What are the situations in which you often experience debilitative emotions?

_____

_____

2. What irrational beliefs do you subscribe to most often? Label them and explain.

_____

_____

_____

3. How can you think more rationally to reduce the number and intensity of irrational emotions? (Give specific examples related to other aspects of your life, as well as referring to the activating events you have described in this exercise.)

_____

_____

_____

_____

ACTIVATING EVENT	SELF-TALK	BASED ON ANY IRRATIONAL FALLACIES?	EMOTION(S)	DISPUTE IRRATIONAL THINKING AND PROVIDE ALTERNATIVE INTERPRETATION
EXAMPLE getting ready for job interview	"The employer will probably ask me a question I can't answer. I'll probably blow the interview. I'll never get a good job – it's hopeless!"	catastrophic failure overgeneralization helplessness	apprehension	There's certainly a *chance* that I'll blow the interview, but there's at least as good a chance that I'll do all right. I'm going overboard when I tell myself that there's no hope. The smartest idea is to do my best and not create a self-fulfilling prophecy of failing.
1.				
2.				
3.				
4.				
5.				

NAME _____

4.6   MEDIATED MESSAGES—EXPRESSING EMOTION

❖ Activity Type: Group Discussion

PURPOSE
To evaluate the expression of emotion in mediated contexts.

INSTRUCTIONS
Discuss each of the questions below in your group. Prepare written answers for your instructor, or be prepared to contribute to a large group discussion, comparing your experiences with those of others in your class.

1. How successful are you at recognizing the emotional dimension of messages from others that are communicated via mediated channels such as written notes, e-mail, telephone, instant messaging/chat? Compare this success with that of others in your group.

   _____

   _____

   _____

2. Mediated contexts may make emotional expression more difficult (lack of touch or facial expression to communicate your happiness). On the other hand, mediated contexts may make emotional expression easier (writing a note to survivors upon the death of someone rather than facing them, for example). Discuss which mediated contexts are most suited to the expression of emotion. Give examples from your own life.

   _____

   _____

   _____

3. In written communication, some stylistic devices (underlining; exclamation marks; emoticons such as the smiley, winking, or sad face) indicate emotion. Evaluate the effectiveness of these substitutions for the vocal and facial expressions of emotion.

   _____

   _____

   _____

NAME _____

4.7   YOUR CALL—EXPRESSING EMOTION

❖ Activity Type: Group Discussion

PURPOSE

To evaluate differences in emotional expression and the effect on a relationship.

INSTRUCTIONS

Use the case below and the discussion questions that follow to discuss the variety of communication issues involved in effective communication. Make notes on this page, add other pages on your own, or prepare a group report/analysis based on your discussion. Add your own experiences to individualize the analysis to make it "Your Call."

CASE

Marcos and Alessandra have been dating for over a year. They love each other and are considering marriage, but each person has at least one big reservation about the other. Marcos thinks Alessandra is moody; it seems that one minute she is "up" and happy with everyone, including him, and the next she criticizes everything about him. Alessandra finds Marcos difficult because he seems to keep everything inside; she wants him to tell her in detail when he feels good and bad, but he says nothing or responds with only a few words.

1. What do you think is the appropriate level of emotional expression between committed partners? Do you think either Marcos or Alessandra should change the way he or she expresses emotions?

    _____

    _____

2. Do you think Marcos and Alessandra each perceive the emotional state of the other accurately? Are there any influences on emotional expression that might exist here (culture, gender, social conventions, social roles, emotional contagion, fear of self-disclosure)?

    _____

    _____

3. Can you identify any irrational fallacies that either Marcos or Alessandra might be following that trigger debilitative emotions?

    _____

    _____

4. What would you recommend that Marcos and Alessandra do about their emotional expressions to improve the quality of their relationship?

_____

_____

STUDY GUIDE

CROSSWORD PUZZLE

Across

4 emotions that prevent a person from functioning effectively

5 basic emotions

8 a fallacy of thinking that believes that acceptance is needed from others

9 interpretations that are the thoughts that accompany strong emotions

11 reactions that are the visible physical signs in response to strong emotions

12 this behaviour could certainly be the result of a debilitating emotion, given its intensity and one's inability to function because of it

Down

1 the nonvocal process of thinking

2 emotions that are combinations of primary emotions

3 emotions that contribute to effective functioning

5 these result in our tendency to avoid expressing emotions verbally, especially negative ones

6 stimuli that are sensations activated by movement of internal tissues

7 referring to other life situations is one of the four verbal ways to describe and express an emotion

10 the length of an emotion

TRUE/FALSE

Mark the statements below as true or false. Correct statements that are false on the lines below to create a true statement.

_____ 1. According to Zimbardo's survey of shyness, people who labelled themselves "not shy" behaved in virtually the same way as those people who labelled themselves "shy" in certain social situations.

_____

_____ 2. Research supports the position that both non-expression and over-expression of emotions are potentially bad for your health.

_____

_____ 3. Daniel Goleman identified a wide range of benefits for people who can't talk about their emotions.

_____

_____ 4. In mainstream North American society, the unwritten rules of communication encourage the direct expression of most emotions.

_____

_____ 5. "I feel confined" is an emotional counterfeit statement.

_____

_____ 6. By rationally disputing your debilitating emotions, you will be able to completely eliminate them from your life.

_____

_____ 7. A certain amount of negative emotion can be constructive or facilitative.

_____

_____ 8. It's the interpretations people make of events that cause their feelings.

_____

_____ 9. When we stop buying into the fallacy of approval, we will be free of any concern about what other people think of us.

_____

_____ 10. We should express all our feelings to the really important people in our life as soon as we feel them.

_____

CHAPTER 5

Language: Barrier and Bridge

OUTLINE

Use this outline to take notes as you read the chapter in the text and/or as your instructor lectures in class.

I.   The nature of language

    A.   Language Is Symbolic

    B.   Language Is Subjective

    C.   Language Is Rule-Governed

        1. Phonological rules

        2. Syntactic rules

        3. Semantic rules

        4. Pragmatic rules – CMM theory

II.   The impact of language

    A.   Naming and Identity

    B.   Affiliation, Attraction, and Interest

        1. Convergence

        2. Divergence

        3. Liking/interest

            a.   Demonstrative pronoun choice

            b.   Sequential placement

            c.   Negation

            d.   Duration

    C.   Power

III.   Uses (and abuses) of language

A.   Precision and Vagueness

1. Equivocation
2. Abstraction
   a. High-abstraction advantages
      1) Shorthand
      2) Avoiding confrontation
      3) Avoiding embarrassment
   b. High-abstraction problems
      1) Stereotyping
      2) Confusing others
      3) Confusing yourself
      4) Lack of relational clarity
   c. Specific behavioural language
      1) The participants
      2) The circumstances
      3) The behaviours
3. Euphemism
4. Relative language
5. Static evaluation

B.   The Language of Responsibility

1. "It" statements
2. "But" statements
3. Questions
4. "I" and "you" language
   a. "I" language
      1) Describes behaviour
      2) Describes feelings
      3) Describes consequences
   b. Advantages of "I" language
      1) Defence reduction
      2) Honesty
      3) Completeness
   c. Problems with "I" language
      1) Anger interferes
      2) Other still gets defensive
      3) Can sound artificial
5. "We" language
   a. Builds constructive climate
   b. Can sound presumptuous

C.   Disruptive language

1. Fact-opinion confusion
2. Fact-inference confusion
3. Emotive language

IV.   Gender and language

A.   Content
1. Some common topics
2. Sex talk restricted to same gender
3. Many topics vary by gender

B.   Reasons for Communicating
1. Women – establish and maintain relationships
   a. Support
   b. Questions
   c. Frequency
2. Men – accomplish tasks
   a. Control
   b. Competition
   c. Practical value

C.   Conversational Style

D.   Other Variables Related to Gender
1. Social orientation
2. Occupation
3. Sex roles

V.   Language and culture

A.   Verbal Communication Styles
1. Low-context/high-context (level of directness)
2. Elaborate/succinct
3. Formal/informal

B.   Language and Worldview
1. Linguistic determinism
2. Sapir–Whorf hypothesis
3. Linguistic relativism

KEY TERMS

Use these key terms to review major concepts from your text. Write the definition for each key term in the space to the right.

abstraction ladder _____

abstractions _____

behavioural description _____

"but" statement _____

CMM theory _____

convergence _____

deferential _____

directness _____

disclaimers _____

divergence _____

elaborate _____

emotive language _____

equivocal language _____

euphemisms _____

fact-inference confusion _____

fact-opinion confusion _____

formality _____

hedges _____

hesitations _____

high-context cultures _____

"I" language _____

informality _____

intensifiers _____

"it" statements _____

language markers _____

language of power _____

language of responsibility _____

linguistic determinism _____

linguistic relativism _____

low-context cultures _____

phonological rules _____

polite forms _____

powerless speech mannerisms _____

pragmatic rules _____

relative language _____

Sapir–Whorf hypothesis _____

semantic rules _____

sex roles _____

static evaluation _____

stereotyping _____

subscripting _____

succinct _____

syntactic rules _____

tag questions _____

"we" statements _____

"you" language _____

NAME _____

ACTIVITIES

5.1   LABEL THE LANGUAGE

❖ Activity Type: Skill Builder

PURPOSE
To help you recognize and change the imprecise language described in Chapter 5 of *Looking Out/Looking In*.

INSTRUCTIONS
1. In groups, label the language contained in each of the sentences below as relative language, emotive terms, or equivocal language.
2. Rewrite each sentence in more precise language.
3. Write your own examples of each variety of language in the space provided.
4. Compare your answers with those of the other groups.

EXAMPLE
I'm trying to diet, so give me a **small piece of cake.**

Language *Relative language*
Revised statement *I'm trying to diet, so give me a piece of cake about half the size of yours.*

1. I don't like the **way things are going**.

   Language _____

   Revised statement _____

   _____

2. He's **so cheap**!

   Language _____

   Revised statement _____

   _____

3. Kali's a real **nuisance**.

   Language _____

Revised statement _____

_____

4. Our candidate is trying to bring about a more **peaceful** world.

Language _____

Revised statement _____

_____

5. Make sure you put in **lots of effort**.

Language _____

Revised statement _____

_____

6. Your essay should be **brief**.

Language _____

Revised statement _____

_____

7. She's a very **mature** child for her age.

Language _____

Revised statement _____

_____

8. Your contribution will help make government **more responsible to the people**.

Language _____

Revised statement _____

_____

9. You know **what's best**.

Language _____

Revised statement _____

_____

10. Bob is really **obsessive** about getting his assignments in on time.

    Language _____

    Revised statement _____

    _____

11. Her standards are just **too high**.

    Language _____

    Revised statement _____

    _____

12. We need to make some **changes** around here.

    Language _____

    Revised statement _____

    _____

13. She was **higher than a kite**!

    Language _____

    Revised statement _____

    _____

14. You weren't **very helpful**.

    Language _____

    Revised statement _____

    _____

15. He's **prejudiced**.

    Language _____

    Revised statement _____

    _____

16. Please leave **a brief message**.

Language _____

Revised statement _____

_____

17. You've got **really poor attendance**.

Language _____

Revised statement _____

_____

18. She is **too uptight**.

Language _____

Revised statement _____

_____

Now write your own examples of each type of language and revise the statements to illustrate alternative language.

19. Equivocal language _____

_____

Revised _____

_____

20. Relative language _____

_____

Revised _____

_____

21. Emotive language _____

_____

Revised _____

_____

NAME _____

5.2   BEHAVIOURAL DESCRIPTIONS

❖ Activity Type: Skill Builder

PURPOSE
To increase the clarity of your language by using behavioural descriptions.

INSTRUCTIONS
In each of the situations below, describe the behaviour of an individual that might have led to the statement about him or her.

EXAMPLES

Hamid's full of action.
Hamid rode his bike for an hour and then mowed the lawn.

Juliana is so much fun to be with.
Juliana went shopping in the mall with me and laughed with me about how we looked in the new, looser styles.

1.   That teacher is a bore!

    _____

    _____

2.   That guy's real macho.

    _____

    _____

3.   She's an all-around good person.

    _____

    _____

4.   Aaron just doesn't seem to care.

    _____

    _____

5. Mark's real laid-back.

_____

_____

6. Zak's really full of himself.

_____

_____

7. Josh is a real sport.

_____

_____

8. She gives me moral support.

_____

_____

9. Jacque's motivated.

_____

_____

10. Alana is inspiring.

_____

_____

11. My boss really needs to lighten up.

_____

_____

12. Yasmin's a flake!

_____

_____

13. You're too emotional.

_____

_____

14. He's so thoughtful.

_____

_____

NAME _____

5.3   LANGUAGE CLARITY

◆ Activity Type: Skill Builder

PURPOSE
To increase the clarity of your language by revising phrases to describe an idea or act.

INSTRUCTIONS
For each of the statements below, write a clear description of the idea or act to clarify to an imagined partner your intentions. Record examples of your own at the end of the exercise.

EXAMPLE
"Go over that way."
"Go across the footbridge, turn right, and go to the third building on your left."

1. "Clean up your act."

    _____

    _____

2. "This time, clean the car correctly."

    _____

    _____

3. "Look more confident."

    _____

    _____

4. "You add a bit of this and that and the sauce is finished."

    _____

    _____

5. "This paper should be creative."

_____

_____

6. "Make that report clearer."

_____

_____

7. "Work harder on your studies."

_____

_____

8. "Pay more attention."

_____

_____

9. "Don't be so obnoxious!"

_____

_____

10. "Don't say things like that."

_____

_____

11. "Clean up your room."

_____

_____

12. "Be kind to your sister."

_____

_____

13. "Get something good at the video store."

_____

_____

14. "Fix a healthy dinner."

_____

_____

15. "Show me that you care."

_____

_____

16. "Your language is too pushy around my family."

_____

_____

17. "You'll never get anywhere in the company talking like that."

_____

_____

18. "You talk like a child."

_____

_____

Now record unclear directions of your own and rewrite them with clear descriptions.

19. _____

_____

_____

20. _____

_____

_____

NAME _____

5.4   PRACTISING "I" LANGUAGE

◆❖ Activity Type: Skill Builder

PURPOSE
To give you practice speaking descriptively, instead of evaluatively.

INSTRUCTIONS
1. Rewrite each of the evaluative "you" language statements below using descriptive "I" language. Be careful to
   a. use specific, low-level abstractions.
   b. take responsibility for your own thoughts and feelings (don't say "I feel you are. . .").
   c. avoid loaded terms "you wouldn't *even*," "you could *at least*," *finally, whenever, ever since,* etc.
2. Record examples of your own at the end and rewrite them.

EXAMPLES

"You don't care about my feelings."
"I felt hurt when I saw you in the restaurant with your old girlfriend after you had told me you had to work."

"That was a dumb move!"
"Ever since you used the high setting to dry my favourite cotton shirt, it doesn't fit me anymore. That's why I'm so angry."

1. "You never want to hear my side of the story."

   _____

   _____

   _____

2. "You don't keep your word."

   _____

   _____

   _____

3. "You're no fun."

_____

_____

_____

4. "You can't take a joke."

_____

_____

_____

5. "Do you ever tell the truth?"

_____

_____

_____

6. "You exaggerate things."

_____

_____

_____

7. "You're making me crazy!"

_____

_____

_____

8. "You have a bad attitude."

_____

_____

_____

9. "You aren't there for me."

_____

_____

_____

10. "You ruined my day."

_____

_____

_____

11. "You're always in a bad mood."

_____

_____

_____

12. "You can never do anything because you always work."

_____

_____

_____

Record your own "you" language statements here. Rewrite them using "I" language.

13. _____.

_____

_____

14. _____.

_____

_____

15. _____.

_____

_____

NAME _____

5.5   "I" LANGUAGE

❖ Activity Type: Oral Skill

PURPOSE
To evaluate your skill in delivering "I" language statements.

INSTRUCTIONS
1. Form partners and identify situations in your lives in which both "you" and "I" language messages might be delivered.
2. Deliver in a realistic manner both a "you" message and an "I" message to your partner according to Chapter 5 of *Looking Out/Looking In* and outlined in the checklist below.
3. Describe on a separate sheet of paper
    a. how well "I" language might (or might not) work in the situation you have chosen. If you do not think "I" language is the best approach for this situation, explain why and describe a more promising alternative.
    b. the degree to which you could (or could not) increase your communicative competence by using "I" language in other situations.

CHECKLIST

_____   Delivers a "you" message to partner.

_____   Delivers the same message in "I" language, without using notes.

        _____   Describes the other's specific behaviour(s) in specific, behaviour terms, using non-evaluative language.

        _____   Describes own feelings arising from other's behaviour(s).

        _____   Describes consequences of other's behaviour(s) as appropriate for self, for the other person, for third parties, or for the relationship.

_____   Verbal and nonverbal behaviour.

        _____   Reflects responsibility for "owning" the message.

        _____   Sounds realistic and consistent with personal style.

_____   Evaluates probable outcome of "I" message, explaining how it might be used or adapted in this and other real-life situations.

NAME _____

5.6   MEDIATED MESSAGES—LANGUAGE

❖ Activity Type: Group Discussion

PURPOSE
To analyze the use of language in mediated contexts.

INSTRUCTIONS
Discuss each of the questions below in your group. Prepare written answers for your instructor, or be preapared to contribute to a large group discussion, comparing your experiences with those of others in your class.

1. Your textbook points out that our identity is tied to the names we use. Discuss whether the name(s) you use in mediated contexts makes a difference (e.g., your e-mail address or your chat-room identity).

   _____

   _____

2. The language used in an answering-machine or voice-mail message can be very formal or very informal. Discuss the pros and cons of formal versus informal mediated messages. Does the language that people use make a difference?

   _____

   _____

3. Sometimes people "talk" in mediated channels just as they would face-to-face. At times this is appropriate, but at other times, language should be adapted to the media (e.g., you get a five-minute voice mail that should have been summarized in 30 seconds).

   _____

   _____

4. What gender or social role differences have you noticed in the *language* of mediated communication? (Example: *My son seems much more comfortable "talking" about emotions through e-mail, whereas my daughter prefers the telephone. I wonder if others experience this.*) (Example: *When my husband's secretary sends me an e-mail, she addresses me using very informal language that she never uses with me face-to-face.*)

   _____

   _____

NAME _____

5.7   YOUR CALL—LANGUAGE

❖ Activity Type: Group Discussion

PURPOSE

To analyze language choices and their effect on a relationship.

INSTRUCTIONS

Use the case below and the discussion questions that follow to discuss the variety of communication issues involved in effective communication. Make notes on this page, add other pages of your own, or prepare a group report/analysis based on your discussion. Add your own experiences to individualize the analysis to make it "Your Call."

CASE

Professor Segura paired Takako and Magdalena as class project partners. After three weeks both Takako and Magdalena came to see Professor Segura, each complaining about the other. Takako called Magdalena a "flake" and said she didn't work hard enough and didn't take the project seriously. Magdalena said that Takako was "arrogant," wanted the project done only her way, and didn't care about all the commitments Magalena had. It is too late in the semester for Professor Segura to give them new partners.

1. What do you think about the language that Takako and Magdalena are using about one another? What effect do you think these types of lanuage have on the successful completion of their project?.

    _____

    _____

2. What high-level abstractions are Takako and Magdalena using? How could they use specific language to improve their situation?

    _____

    _____

3. Do you think the use of "I" language could improve this situation? Give examples of "I" language here.

    _____

    _____

4. Examine any gender or cultural influences that might exist here. Does it matter if both are of the same or different gender or culture? If you can locate language differences, whose responsibility is it to adapt language choices?

    _____

    _____

STUDY GUIDE

CROSSWORD PUZZLE

Across

2   a culture within which the members look more to the circumstances of communication for its meaning

3   a role that is the social orientation that governs language behaviour, rather than the biological gender

5   language that conveys the sender's attitude rather than simply offering an objective description

9   a range of more to less specificity describing an event or object

12 rules of language that govern what meaning language has, as opposed to what structure it has

13 a type of question that is placed in a statement and that leaves the impression the speaker lacks confidence

14 the group of speech mannerisms referred to as deferential because they reduce the perceived power of the speaker

Down

1   categorizing individuals according to a set of characteristics assumed to belong to all members of a group

3   rules of language that govern the ways symbols can be arranged, as opposed to the meanings of those symbols

4   language statement that expresses or implies a judgment of the other person

5   language that consists of words that have more than one commonly accepted definition

6   a pleasant term substituted for a blunt one in order to soften the impact of unpleasant information

7   rules of language that govern how sounds are combined to form words

8   a type of statement that allows the speaker to avoid taking ownership of the message

10 descriptions that refer only to observable phenomena

11 language terms that gain their meaning by comparison

MATCHING

Match the terms in column 1 with their definitions in column 2.

_____ **1.** abstraction ladder

_____ **2.** behavioural description

_____ **3.** equivocal language

_____ **4.** emotive language

_____ **5.** euphemisms

_____ **6.** high-context cultures

_____ **7.** low-context cultures

_____ **8.** "I" language

_____ **9.** linguistic determinism

_____ **10.** linguistic relativism

_____ **11.** relative language

_____ **12.** semantic rules

_____ **13.** phonological rules

_____ **14.** pragmatic rules

_____ **15.** Sapir–Whorf hypothesis

_____ **16.** static evaluation

_____ **17.** stereotyping

_____ **18.** syntactic rules

_____ **19.** "you" language

_____ **20.** sex role

a. ambiguous language that has two or more equally plausible meanings

b. cultures that avoid direct use of language, relying on the context of a message to convey meaning

c. an account that refers only to observable phenomena

d. cultures that use language primarily to express thoughts, feelings, and ideas as clearly and logically as possible

e. a statement that describes the speaker's reaction to another person's behaviour without making judgments about its worth

f. a range of more or less abstract terms describing an event or object

g. language that conveys the sender's attitude rather than simply offering an objective description

h. pleasant terms substituted for blunt ones in order to soften the impact of unpleasant information

i. a moderate theory that argues that language exerts a strong influence on the perceptions of the people who speak it

j. govern what meaning language has, as opposed to what structure it has

k. the theory that a culture's worldview is unavoidably shaped and reflected by the language its members speak

l. govern how sounds are combined to form words

m. theory of linguistic determinism in which language is determined by a culture's perceived reality

n. language terms that gain their meaning by comparison

o. categorizing individuals according to a set of characteristics assumed to belong to all members of a group

p. govern what interpretation of a message is appropriate in a given context

q. govern the ways symbols can be arranged, as opposed to the meanings of those symbols

r. the social orientation that governs language behaviour, rather than the biological gender

s. the tendency to view people or relationships as unchanging

t. a statement that expresses or implies a judgment of the other person

TRUE/FALSE

Mark the statements below as true or false. For statements that are false, correct them on the lines below to create a true statement.

_____   **1.** Words are not arbitrary symbols; they have meaning in and of themselves.

_____

_____   **2.** According to research, your name is likely to affect people's first impressions of you.

_____

_____   **3.** Since research shows that people are rated as more competent when their talk is free of deferential language markers, it is obvious that a consistently powerful style of speaking is always the best approach.

_____

_____   **4.** Ambiguity and vagueness are forms of language that are to be avoided at all costs.

_____

_____   **5.** Intensifiers are one example of a deferential language marker.

_____

_____   **6.** "How are we feeling today?" is an example of "we" language.

_____

_____   **7.** "Liberals are more responsive to the people than Conservatives are" is an example of a fact statement.

_____

_____   **8.** According to research on language and gender, on the average, men discuss with men different topics than women discuss with other women.

_____

_____   **9.** Inferences and interpretations have quite different meanings.

_____

_____   **10.** A person from Canada is more likely to value direct language than is someone from Japan.

_____

_____ **19.** Franco is the **most wonderful friend**.

    a. Franco has never told anyone about my fear of failing.
    b. Franco listens to me about everything.
    c. Franco is the best listener I've ever met.
    d. I can trust Franco implicitly with all my secrets.

_____ **20.** Keiko **goes overboard** in trying to make people like her.

    a. Keiko gave everyone on the team a valentine.
    b. Keiko is the biggest kiss-up you ever met.
    c. I think Keiko is trying to make my friends like her better than me.
    d. I want Keiko to stop trying to outdo everybody else.

STUDY GUIDE ANSWERS

CROSSWORD PUZZLE

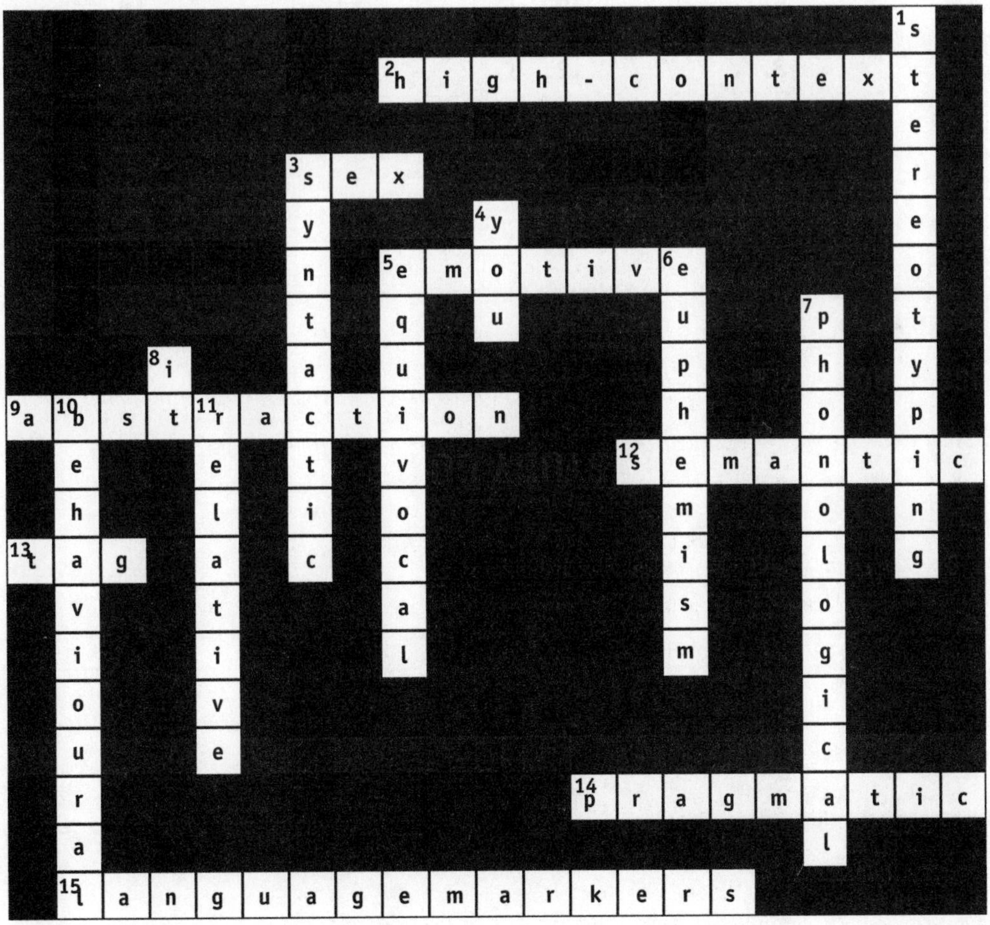

The completed crossword puzzle contains the following answers:

- 1 Down: stereotyping
- 2 Across: high-context
- 3 Down: syntactic
- 4 Down: you
- 5 Across: emotive
- 6 Down: euphemism
- 7 Down: phonological
- 8 Down: i
- 9 Across: a
- 10 Down: behaviourla
- 11 Down: relative
- 14 Across: abstraction
- 12 Across: semantic
- 13 Across: tag
- 14 Across: pragmatic
- 15 Across: language markers

MATCHING

1. f	**5.** h	**9.** k	**13.** l	**17.** o
2. c	**6.** b	**10.** i	**14.** p	**18.** q
3. a	**7.** d	**11.** n	**15.** m	**19.** t
4. g	**8.** e	**12.** j	**16.** s	**20.** r

TRUE/FALSE

1. F	**3.** F	**5.** T	**7.** F	**9.** F
2. T	**4.** F	**6.** F	**8.** T	**10.** T

COMPLETION

1. convergence
2. euphemisms
3. polite forms
4. divergence
5. equivocation
6. tag questions
7. hedges
8. subscripting
9. syntactic rules
10. emotive language

MULTIPLE CHOICE

1. a	**5.** e	**9.** a	**13.** b	**17.** b
2. c	**6.** c	**10.** d	**14.** d	**18.** d
3. b	**7.** e	**11.** c	**15.** c	**19.** a
4. d	**8.** c	**12.** b	**16.** a	**20.** a

CHAPTER 6

Nonverbal Communication: Messages without Words

OUTLINE

Use this outline to take notes as you read the chapter in the text and/or as your instructor lectures in class.

I. Nonverbal communication

    A. Importance

        1. Emotional impact

        2. Greater percentage of social meaning

    B. Definition: Those Messages Expressed by Other Than Linguistic Means

II. Characteristics of nonverbal communication

    A. Nonverbal Communication Exists

    B. Nonverbal Behaviour Has Communicative Value

        1. Deliberate

        2. Unintentional

    C. Nonverbal Communication Is Culture-Bound

    D. Nonverbal Communication Can Differ by Gender

    E. Nonverbal Communication Is Primarily Relational

        1. Identity management

        2. Definition of relationships we want with others

        3. Conveyance of emotion

    F. Nonverbal Communication Serves Many Functions

        1. Repeating

        2. Substituting

        3. Complementing

        4. Accenting

        5. Regulating

      6. Contradicting

  G. **Nonverbal Communication Is Ambiguous**

III. Types of nonverbal communication

A. **Body Orientation**

B. **Posture**
    1. Forward/backward lean
    2. Tension/relaxation

C. **Gestures**
    1. Preening behaviours
    2. Manipulators

D. **Face and Eyes**
    1. Complexity
    2. Speed
    3. Emotions reflected
    4. Microexpression
    5. Kinds of messages
        a. Involvement
        b. Positive/negative attitude
        c. Dominance/submission
        d. Interest (pupils)

E. **Voice (Paralanguage): Tone, Speed, Pitch, Number and Length of Pauses, Volume, Disfluencies**

F. **Touch**

G. **Physical Attractiveness**

H. **Clothing**

I. **Distance**
    1. Intimate
    2. Personal
    3. Social
    4. Public

J. **Territoriality**

K. **Physical Environment**

L. **Time**

IV. Differences between verbal and nonverbal communication

A. **Single versus Multiple Channels**

B. **Intermittent versus Continuous**

C. **Clear versus Ambiguous**

D. **Verbal versus Nonverbal Impact**

E. **Deliberate versus Unconscious**

KEY TERMS

Use these key terms to review major concepts from your text. Write the definition for each key term in the space to the right.

accenting _____

adaptors _____

affect blends _____

body orientation _____

chronemics _____

complementing _____

contradicting _____

deception cues _____

disfluencies _____

double messages _____

emblems _____

emoticons _____

gestures _____

illustrators _____

intimate distance _____

kinesics _____

leakage _____

manipulators _____

microexpression _____

nonverbal communication _____

paralanguage _____

personal distance _____

posture _____

proxemics _____

public distance _____

regulating _____

repeating _____

social distance _____

substituting _____

tension cue _____

territory _____

NAME _____

ACTIVITIES

6.1 DESCRIBING NONVERBAL STATES

❖ Activity Type: Skill Builder

PURPOSE

To describe the nonverbal behaviours that indicate various emotional and attitudinal states.

INSTRUCTIONS

NOTE: Group members (or individuals) may want to make videotaped examples of their own behaviour reflecting each of the situations below or they may want to collect television or movie examples illustrating the emotions and attitudes described below.

1. For each of the statements below, record the nonverbal behaviours that reflect the attitude or emotions described.
2. Compare your responses with those of others in the class and note the similarities and differences in your responses.

STATEMENT	NONVERBAL BEHAVIOUR
EXAMPLE She listens well.	Turns body toward me, leans forward, smiles once or twice, nods, maintains eye contact about 80 percent of the time.
1. He's so insecure.	
2. She's very determined.	
3. He's paranoid.	
4. She seems unsure of what she wants.	

STATEMENT	NONVERBAL BEHAVIOUR
5. He's stressing out.	
6. She's kind of judgmental.	
7. He's overdramatic.	
8. She acts confidently.	
9. He's a bit uptight.	
10. She seems self-conscious.	

COMPARISONS

Record the similarities and differences you found when comparing your responses to those of your classmates.

_____

_____

_____

_____

NAME _____

6.2   NONVERBAL COMPLAINTS

❖ Activity Type: Skill Builder

PURPOSE
To facilitate the display of nonverbally congruent behaviours.

INSTRUCTIONS
1. For each statement in the following chart, describe the nonverbal behaviours that might satisfy the person making the complaint.
2. At the same time, note the type of situation in which you consciously or unconsciously placed the dialogue (e.g., What's going on? Where? Who's involved?).
3. After completing the examples provided, compare your advice with that of others in the class, noting the effects that different people or contexts may have on the advice. Record your answers below.

Compare your advice with that of others in the class. Note any similarities or differences.

_____

_____

_____

_____

How might the persons involved or the context change the advice you would give?

_____

_____

_____

_____

_____

_____

COMPLAINT	NONVERBAL ADVICE	SITUATION SURROUNDING THE DIALOGUE
EXAMPLE He says I'm too eager to please.	Take a little more time to respond after a request. Lean toward the person a little less. Smile, but don't keep the smile on your face continuously. Gesture, but don't gesture as quickly. Stand a little more erect and hold all the parts of your body more still.	I imagined this as a co-worker's advice about how to deal with a particularly domineering supervisor.
1. She says I'm too serious.		
2. He says not to be so aggressive.		
3. He says I could be more helpful.		
4. He says that I don't seem to care.		
5. She says that I don't sound very sure of myself.		
6. They look so sure of themselves, but I just can't act that way.		

COMPLAINT	NONVERBAL ADVICE	SITUATION SURROUNDING THE DIALOGUE
7. I'd like to look more relaxed.		
8. He says that people have commented that I don't look as if I want to be there.		
9. She says I act too cold.		
10. He says I should be more open.		

NAME _____

6.3   SHOW AND TELL

❖ Activity Type: Skill Builder

PURPOSES

1. To practise describing another person's nonverbal communication behaviours specifically.
2. To receive descriptive feedback about some of your own nonverbal behaviours.

INSTRUCTIONS

1. Pair up with another student whom you know well or at least see on a regular basis.
2. Identify an emotion that you think you have seen the other person display on occasion. If you have difficulty thinking of one, some possibilities are listed below. (Alternatively, your partner could tell you which emotion he or she would like you to focus on.)

    Possible emotions:

anger	confidence	apathy	enthusiasm
unhappiness	happiness	contentment	defensiveness
frustration	uncertainty	edginess	agitation
embarrassment	friendliness	hysteria	discouragement
worry	hurt	tiredness	

3. Using the form below, record the specific nonverbal behaviours your partner uses when he or she feels that particular emotion. Record them according to the category of behaviour under which they fall. This may involve all or only some of the different channels.
4. Reverse roles and repeat steps 1–3.

Partner's name _____   Emotion _____

CHANNELS	BEHAVIOURS
Facial expressions	
Gestures	
Postures	
Body orientation	
Distance	
Voice	
Territoriality	
Touch	

NAME _____

6.4   EVALUATING AMBIGUITY

◆ Activity Type: Invitation to Insight

PURPOSES
1. To analyze the verbal and nonverbal aspects of your communication behaviours.
2. To weigh the consequences of sending congruent versus ambiguous messages.

INSTRUCTIONS
1. In each of the situations oulined in the following chart, describe verbal and nonverbal behaviours likely to occur. Use descriptions of the 12 types of nonverbal communication described in Chapter 6 of *Looking Out/Looking In* (i.e., body orientation, posture, gesture, face and eyes, voice, touch, physical attractiveness, clothing, distance, territoriality, physical environment, and time). Nonverbal behaviours seldom occur alone, so describe clusters of at least three nonverbal behaviours for each situation. Note whether the verbal and nonverbal behaviours are ambiguous or congruent (congruent means they send the same, consistent message). Finally, evaluate the possible consequences of the ambiguity or congruency.
2. Next describe five situations from your own life and how you would send verbal and nonverbal messages. Include a brief discussion of the consequences of your congruent or ambiguous behaviours.
3. After you've completed the examples, answer the questions about congruency/ambiguity here.

Consider situations in addition to the examples in this exercise when answering the following questions.

In what situations should you express yourself ambiguously? Explain how sending one message verbally and another one nonverbally could be beneficial.

_____
_____
_____
_____

Describe situations in which ambiguity is not desirable. Describe how you could best match your verbal and nonverbal behaviours in these situations.

_____
_____
_____
_____

SITUATION	YOUR VERBAL BEHAVIOUR	YOUR NONVERBAL BEHAVIOUR (USE A CLUSTER OF BEHAVIOURS HERE)	ARE THE VERBAL/ NONVERBAL MESSAGES AMBIGUOUS?	POSSIBLE CONSEQUENCES
EXAMPLE The person I like a lot takes me out to dinner and I have a good time and enjoy the food.	"I'm really enjoying this; the food is terrific and so is the company."	I look at my partner when I talk, smiling and tilting my head slightly forward. I lean toward my partner and touch my partner lightly on the arm and hand.	My verbal and nonverbal behaviours are not ambiguous in this context.	I hope the consequences are that my partner will understand how much I care and enjoy our time together. I run the risk of not "game playing," of course – in that I could be hurt if my partner's feelings don't match mine – but I think the chances are pretty slim in this instance.
1. My boss asks me to work late when I've made other plans.				
2. My roommate asks, while I'm doing homework, if I can make dinner.				

SITUATION	YOUR VERBAL BEHAVIOUR	YOUR NONVERBAL BEHAVIOUR (USE A CLUSTER OF BEHAVIOURS HERE)	ARE THE VERBAL/ NONVERBAL MESSAGES AMBIGUOUS?	POSSIBLE CONSEQUENCES
3. My relative drops in to visit me when other people are over for the evening.				
4. My lab partner suggests that we go out partying together Friday night.				
5. The waiter grabs my plate and asks if I'm finished while food is still on my plate.				
6.				

SITUATION	YOUR VERBAL BEHAVIOUR	YOUR NONVERBAL BEHAVIOUR (USE A CLUSTER OF BEHAVIOURS HERE)	ARE THE VERBAL/ NONVERBAL MESSAGES AMBIGUOUS?	POSSIBLE CONSEQUENCES
7.				
8.				
9.				
10.				

NAME _____

6.5   MEDIATED MESSAGES—NONVERBAL COMMUNICATION

❖ Activity Type: Group Discussion

PURPOSE
To analyze nonverbal communication in mediated contexts.

INSTRUCTIONS
Discuss each of the questions below in your group. Prepare written answers for your instructor or be prepared to contribute to a large group discussion, comparing your experiences with those of others in your class.

1. Mediated contexts often deprive us of important nonverbal communication cues. Discuss what nonverbal cues are present and absent in the mediated contexts (e.g., telephone, e-mail, handwritten messages) used by members of your group.

   _____

   _____

2. Discuss the substitutions that people make for missing nonverbal cues in mediated contexts. How can you compensate to express yourself and understand others most fully when nonverbal cues aren't available in mediated communication?

   _____

   _____

3. Your textbook discusses nonverbal signals of deception, or leakage. Do you think it is easier or more difficult to detect deception in mediated contexts?

   _____

   _____

4. The use of time can express both intentional and unintentional messages. Discuss the messages conveyed by the use of time in mediated contexts (e.g., the length of time taken to return a phone call or an e-mail).

   _____

   _____

NAME _____

6.6   YOUR CALL—NONVERBAL BEHAVIOUR

❖ Activity Type: Group Discussion

PURPOSE

To analyze the possible interpretations of specific nonverbal behaviours and how to respond to them.

INSTRUCTIONS

Use the case below and the discussion questions that follow to discuss the variety of communication issues involved in effective communication. Make notes on this page, add other pages on your own, or prepare a group report/analysis based on your discussion. Add your own experiences to individualize the analysis to make it "Your Call."

CASE

Malena and Dolly are co-workers in different departments in a large company. Over coffee one day Malena tells Dolly that she's been feeling very uneasy lately about her boss's behaviour. "I'm not exactly sure how to describe it," Malena says, "but I think he's coming on to me, and I don't know what to do."

1. If Malena decides to report this behaviour, she needs to be able to describe it. Use your knowledge of situations like this to describe the behaviour of Malena's boss.

    _____

    _____

2. Do you think it is possible that Malena may be misinterpreting her boss's behaviour?

    _____

    _____

3. Are there nonverbal behaviours on Malena's part that may contribute to or increase the problem? Describe what they might be.

    _____

    _____

4. If you were Dolly, what would you tell Malena to do verbally and nonverbally to handle this issue?

    _____

    _____

STUDY GUIDE

CROSSWORD PUZZLE

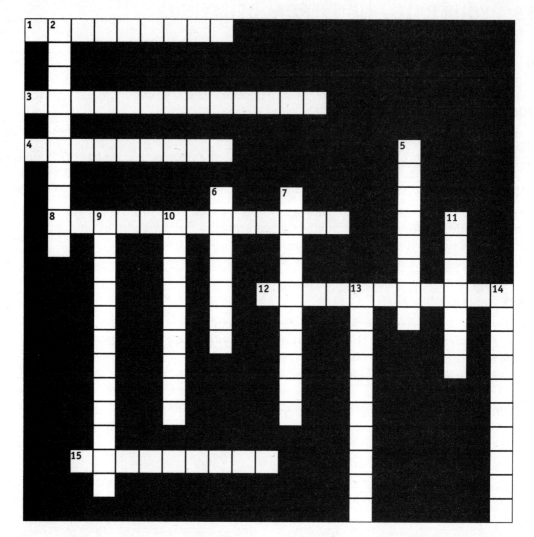

Across

1 nonverbal behaviour that emphasizes part of a verbal message

3 nonverbal behaviour that is inconsistent with a verbal message

4 nonverbal behaviour cues that signal the untruthfulness of a verbal message

8 nonverbal behaviour that reinforces a verbal message

12 nonverbal behaviour that accompanies and supports verbal messages

13 the study of how people and animals use space

Down

2 the study of how humans use and structure time

5 usually unconscious gestures, such as fiddling with one's hair

6 nonverbal behaviours that reveal information a communicator does not disclose verbally

7 a nonlinguistic verbalization like *um, er, ah*

9 movements in which one part of the body grooms, massages, rubs, holds, fidgets, pinches, picks or otherwise manipulates another part

10 a variety of symbols used in e-mail correspondence to simulate the nonverbal dimension of communication

11 the way in which individuals carry themselves: erect, slumping, and so on

13 a nonverbal behaviour that takes the place of the spoken words

14 nonverbal behaviour influencing the flow of verbal communication

TRUE/FALSE

Mark the statements below as true or false. Correct statements that are false on the lines below to create a true statement.

_____   **1.** Touch has been used successfully to help premature babies gain weight.

_____

_____   **2.** Certain nonverbal behaviours like smiling are universal, and thus they are used and interpreted similarly around the world.

_____

_____   **3.** The concept of nonverbal convergence illustrates that skilled communicators can adapt their behaviour when interacting with members of other cultures or subcultures in order to make the exchange more smooth and effective.

_____

_____   **4.** Nonverbal communication is much better suited to expressing attitudes and feelings than it is to expressing ideas.

_____

_____   **5.** The only time we stop communicating nonverbally is in our sleep.

_____

_____   **6.** In studies of detecting lying, men are consistently more accurate than women at detecting the lies and discovering the underlying truth.

_____

_____   **7.** In the Western world, men make more eye contact than women when having a conversation.

_____

_____   **8.** Unlike verbal communication that is discrete (has a clear beginning and end), nonverbal communication is continuous and never ending.

_____

_____   **9.** The nonverbal impact of messages is more powerful than the verbal impact.

_____

_____   **10.** Nonverbal communication is clearer than verbal communication.

_____

COMPLETION

Fill in the blanks below with the correct terms chosen from the list below.

leakage	personal	disfluencies	public	relaxation
paralanguage	emblem	affect blend	microexpression	body orientation

1. _____ are the normal stammers and *ums* of speaking.

2. _____ is a postural cue such as leaning back or lowering shoulders that a higher-status person usually exhibits when not feeling threatened.

3. _____ is a deliberate, nonverbal behaviour that has a very precise meaning known to virtually everyone within a cultural group.

4. _____ is the distance zone identified by Hall that ranges from 45 cm to 1.2 m and includes behaviour found in most social conversations.

5. _____ is the combination of two or more expressions in different parts of the face.

6. _____ is the degree to which we face toward or away from someone with our body, feet, and head.

7. _____ is a fleeting change in nonverbal communication that is inconsistent with the speaker's intended message.

8. _____ is the distance zone identified by Hall that ranges from 3.6 m outward and includes communication such as that found in a typical classroom.

9. _____ is nonverbal behaviour that includes having a foreign accent.

10. _____ is when our nonverbal behaviour signals our attempt at deception.

MULTIPLE CHOICE

Choose the letter of the type of nonverbal communication that is illustrated below.

a. environment   b. paralinguistics   c. proxemics   d. territoriality

_____   1. After a while, all the guests had definitely established "their" spots at the dinner table.

_____   2. Josh kept the door to his bedroom closed when he didn't want to be disturbed.

_____   3. The first thing Christine did in her new house was put a welcome mat on the front step.

_____   4. Karen really likes to sit close to Harry when they watch movies.

_____   5. When Jessica and Ian fight, they try to stay away from each other as much as they can.

_____ **6.** Sanjay's voice softened when he spoke to her.

_____ **7.** There was a long pause after the decision was made.

_____ **8.** Mitchell sighed audibly.

_____ **9.** Gretchen took the third seat down from Yayoi.

_____ **10.** Witold was annoyed that someone was leaning on his car.

a. body orientation   b. gestures   c. touch   d. face and eyes

_____ **11.** The children playfully kicked one another.

_____ **12.** Professor D'Angelo illustrated her lecture with many arm movements.

_____ **13.** Leland shifted his shoulders toward the speaker.

_____ **14.** Ernie avoided looking at her.

_____ **15.** The executive stared at her employee.

_____ **16.** Aaron turned his body away from his brother.

_____ **17.** The officer pointed in the correct direction.

_____ **18.** Semareh didn't appreciate the slap on the back.

_____ **19.** Hiroshi set his jaw in disgust.

_____ **20.** Francesca signalled "OK" across the room.

STUDY GUIDE ANSWERS

CROSSWORD PUZZLE

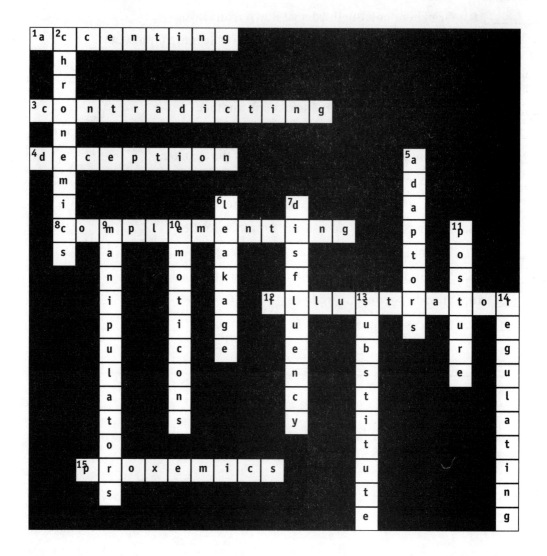

TRUE/FALSE

1. T	**3.** T	**5.** F	**7.** F	**9.** T
2. T	**4.** T	**6.** F	**8.** T	**10.** F

COMPLETION

1. disfluencies
2. relaxation
3. emblem
4. personal
5. affect blend
6. body orientation
7. microexpression
8. public
9. paralanguage
10. leakage

MULTIPLE CHOICE

1. d	**5.** c	**9.** c	**13.** a	**17.** b
2. d	**6.** b	**10.** d	**14.** d	**18.** c
3. a	**7.** b	**11.** c	**15.** d	**19.** d
4. c	**8.** b	**12.** b	**16.** a	**20.** b

CHAPTER 7

Listening: More Than Meets the Ear

OUTLINE

Use this outline to take notes as you read the chapter in the text and/or as your instructor lectures in class.

I. Listening is important

   A. Frequency

   B. Relational Skill

II. Elements in the listening process

   A. Hearing

   B. Attending

   C. Understanding

   D. Responding

   E. Remembering

III. Types of ineffective listening

   A. Pseudolistening

   B. Stage-Hogging

   C. Selective Listening

   D. Insulated Listening

   E. Defensive Listening

   F. Ambushing

   G. Insensitive Listening

IV. Why we don't listen

   A. Message Overload

B. **Preoccupation**

C. **Rapid Thought**

D. **Effort**

E. **External Noise**

F. **Hearing Problems**

G. **Faulty Assumptions**
    1. Heard it all before
    2. Speaker's words too simple
    3. Speaker's words too complex
    4. Subject is uninteresting

H. **Lack of Apparent Advantages**
    1. Control
    2. Admiration/respect
    3. Energy release

I. **Lack of Training**

J. **Media Influences**

V.   Informational listening

A. **Talk Less**

B. **Get Rid of Distractions**

C. **Don't Judge Prematurely**

D. **Look for Key Ideas**

E. **Ask Questions**
    1. Avoid counterfeit questions that
        a. Trap the speaker
        b. Make statements
        c. Carry hidden agendas
        d. Seek "correct" answers
        e. Are based on unchecked assumptions
    2. Ask sincere questions
        a. Clarify thoughts and feelings
        b. Underused
            1) People are reluctant to ask
            2) People think they already understand

F. **Paraphrase**
    1. Change the speaker's wording
    2. Offer an example of what you think the speaker is talking about
    3. Reflect the underlying theme of the speaker's remarks

VI.   Listening to help

A. **Advising: Offering a Solution**
    1. Be accurate

    2. Be sure other is ready to accept

    3. Avoid implying blame

B. Judging: Evaluating

    1. Be sure judgment is asked for

    2. Make judgment constructive

C. Analyzing: Interpreting

    1. Be tentative

    2. Have chance of being correct

    3. Be sure person is receptive

    4. Have desire to help as motive

D. Questioning: Clarifying

    1. Don't ask to satisfy your own curiosity

    2. Don't confuse or distract

    3. Don't disguise suggestions/criticism

E. Supporting: Expressing Solidarity

    1. Types

        a. Agreement

        b. Offers to help

        c. Praise

        d. Reassurance

        e. Diversion

    2. Potential problems

        a. Deny others the right to their feelings

        b. Minimize the situation

        c. Focus on "then and there"

        d. Cast judgment

        e. Defend yourself

        f. Rain on the speaker's parade

    3. Guidelines

        a. Approval not necessary

        b. Monitor reaction

F. Prompting: Encouraging

G. Paraphrasing: Reflecting Understanding

    1. Thoughts

    2. Feelings

    3. When to use paraphrasing

        a. If the problem is complex enough

        b. If you have necessary time and concern

        c. If you are genuinely interested in helping

        d. If you can withhold judgment

        e. If you're comfortable with style and don't overuse it

H. When and How to Help

    1. Consider the situation

    2. Consider the other person

    3. Consider yourself

KEY TERMS

Use these key terms to review major concepts from your text. Write the definition for each key term in the space to the right.

active listening _____

advising response _____

ambushing _____

analyzing statement _____

attending _____

closed questions _____

counterfeit questions _____

defensive listening _____

hearing _____

insensitive listening _____

insulated listening _____

judging response _____

listening _____

open questions _____

paraphrasing _____

prompting _____

pseudolistening _____

questioning response _____

remembering _____

residual message _____

responding _____

selective listening _____

sincere questions _____

stage-hogging _____

supporting response _____

understanding _____

NAME _____

ACTIVITIES

7.1 LISTENING DIARY

◆ Activity Type: Invitation to Insight

PURPOSES

1. To help you identify the styles of listening you use in your interpersonal relation-ships.
2. To help you discover the consequences of the listening styles you use.

BACKGROUND

Looking Out/Looking In identifies several styles of effective and ineffective listening that you can use when seeking information from another:

pseudolistening   insensitive listening
stage-hogging   ambushing
selective listening   prompting
insulated listening   questioning
defensive listening   paraphrasing

INSTRUCTIONS

1. Use the form on the following page to record the listening styles you use in various situations.
2. After completing your diary, record your conclusions here.

Based on your observations, what styles of effective and ineffective listening do you use most often? In what situations do you use each of these styles? (Consider the people involved, the time, subject, and your personal mood when determining situational vari-ables.)

_____

_____

_____

_____

What are the consequences of using the listening styles you have just described?

_____

_____

_____

_____

TIME AND PLACE	PEOPLE	SUBJECT	LISTENING STYLE(S)	CONSEQUENCES
EXAMPLE Saturday night party	my date and several new acquaintances	good backpacking trips	*stage-hogging:* I used everybody's remarks to show what a hotshot explorer I am.	I guess I was trying to get everyone to like me. My egotistical attitude probably accomplished the opposite!
1.				
2.				
3.				

NAME _____

7.2   RESPONSES TO PROBLEMS

❖ Activity Type: Skill Builder

PURPOSE

To help you practise the various styles of responding to others' problems.

INSTRUCTIONS

For each of the problem statements below, write a response in each style of helping discussed in *Looking Out/Looking In*. Make your response as realistic as possible. Then record a situation of your own and write listening responses for it.

EXAMPLE

"I don't know what to do. I tried to explain to my professor why the assignment was late, but he wouldn't even listen to me."

Advising *You ought to write him a note. He might be more open if he has time to read it and think about it.*

Judging *You have to accept these things. Moping won't do any good, so quit feeling sorry for yourself.*

Analyzing *I think the reason he wasn't sympathetic is because he hears lots of excuses this time of year.*

Supporting *All of your work has been so good that I'm sure this one assignment won't matter. Don't worry!*

Questioning *What did he say? Do you think he'll change his mind later? How could you make up the assignment?*

Prompting *(Short silence) And so . . . ?*

Paraphrasing *You sound really discouraged, since he didn't even seem to care about your reasons – is that it?*

1. "My girlfriend says she wants to date other guys this summer while I'm up north working on construction. She claims it's just to keep busy and that it won't make any difference with us, but I think she wants to break off permanently, and she's trying to do it gently."

   Advising _____

   _____

   Judging _____

   _____

Analyzing _____

_____

Supporting _____

_____

Questioning _____

_____

Prompting _____

_____

Paraphrasing _____

_____

2. "I'm setting so sick of group work! At least one person doesn't show up for meetings or shows up late and unprepared. And I always seem to get stuck with more than my share of the workload."

Advising _____

_____

Judging _____

_____

Analyzing _____

_____

Supporting _____

_____

Questioning _____

_____

Prompting _____

_____

Paraphrasing _____

_____

3. "What do you do about a friend who borrows things and doesn't return them?"

Advising _____

_____

Judging _____

_____

Analyzing _____

_____

Supporting _____

_____

Questioning _____

_____

Prompting _____

_____

Paraphrasing _____

_____

4. "The pressure of going to school and doing all the other things in my life is really getting to me. I can't go on like this, but I don't know where I can cut back."

Advising _____

_____

Judging _____

_____

Analyzing _____

_____

Supporting _____

_____

Questioning _____

_____

Prompting _____

_____

Paraphrasing _____

_____

5. "You'd think that by the time you became an adult your parents would stop treating you like a child, but not mine! If I wanted their advice about how to live my life, I'd ask."

Advising _____

_____

Judging _____

_____

Analyzing _____

_____

Supporting _____

_____

Questioning _____

_____

Prompting _____

_____

Paraphrasing _____

_____

Record a situation of your own here

6. _____

_____

Advising _____

_____

Judging _____

_____

Analyzing _____

_____

Supporting _____

_____

Questioning _____

_____

Prompting _____

_____

Paraphrasing _____

_____

NAME _____

7.3   PARAPHRASING PRACTICE

❖ Activity Type: Skill Builder

PURPOSE
To develop your ability to paraphrase in order to gain information about another person's thoughts.

INSTRUCTIONS
Write a paraphrasing response for each of the following statements. Include the speaker's thoughts and, as appropriate, the speaker's feelings. Remember to do at least one of the following to avoid repeating: (1) change the wording, (2) offer an example, and/or (3) look for the underlying theme.

EXAMPLE

"It's not fair that I have to work so much. Other students can get better grades because they have the time to study."
So your job is taking time away from your studies and you think you're at a disadvantage?

1. "I guess it's OK for you to use my computer. Just make sure you handle the disks carefully, and don't put any food or drinks on the desk or anywhere near the machine. This computer cost me a lot of money, and it would be a disaster if anything happened to it."

   _____

   _____

   _____

2. "You'll have the best chance at getting a loan for the new car you want if you give us a complete financial statement and credit history."

   _____

   _____

   _____

3. (Instructor to student) "This paper shows a lot of promise. It could probably earn you an A grade if you just developed the idea about the problems that arise from poor listening a bit more."

_____

_____

_____

4. "I do like the communication course, but it's not at all what I expected. It's much more _personal,_ if you know what I mean."

_____

_____

_____

5. "We just got started on your car's transmission. I'm pretty sure we can have it ready tonight."

_____

_____

_____

6. "I like the new boss but I'm afraid she's going to focus her energy on cutting costs rather than on providing good customer service."

_____

_____

_____

7. "We are planning to have some friends over tonight, but I guess you're welcome to come too. Why don't you just bring along something we can munch on so we'll be sure to have enough food?"

_____

_____

_____

8. "You know I enjoy spending time with you. But I have other friends, too!"

_____

_____

_____

NAME _____

7.4   LISTENING FOR FEELINGS

❖ Activity Type: Skill Builder

PURPOSE

To help you identify the feelings that are often implied but not stated by others.

INSTRUCTIONS

For each of the statements below, write the feeling or feelings that the speaker might be experiencing.

SPEAKER'S REMARKS	POSSIBLE FEELINGS
EXAMPLE It seems like you haven't been paying much attention to me lately. Is there something wrong?	puzzlement, hurt
1. I wonder if I ought to start looking for another job. They're reorganizing the company, and what with a drop in business and all, maybe this is one of the jobs they'll cut back on. But if my boss finds out I'm looking around, maybe he'll think I don't like it here and let me go anyway.	
2. It was a great game. I played a lot, I guess, but I only scored once. The coach put Kyler in ahead of me.	
3. I said I'd do the collecting for him, but I sure don't feel like it. But I owe him a favour, so I guess I'll have to do it.	
4. I've got a report due tomorrow, an exam the next day, rehearsals every night this week, and now a meeting this afternoon. I don't think I can even fit in eating, and this has been going on all month.	
5. Sure she gets better grades than I do. She's a homemaker, takes only two classes, and all she has to do is study. I have to work a job and go to school, too. And I don't have anyone to support me.	

SPEAKER'S REMARKS POSSIBLE FEELINGS	
6. I can't understand why they haven't written. They've never been gone this long without at least a card, and I don't even know how to get in touch with them.	
7. We had a great evening last night. The dinner was fantastic; so was the party. We saw lots of people; Jette loves that sort of thing.	
8. My daughter got straight A's this year, and the high school has a reputation for being very hard. She's a natural student. But sometimes I wish I could help her get interested in something besides studying.	
9. Boy, the teacher tells us he'll deduct marks every time we're late, but it doesn't seem to bother him when he comes in late. He must figure it's his privilege.	
10. I worked up that whole study – did all the surveying, the compiling, the writing. It was my idea in the first place. But he turned it in to the head office with his name on it, and he got the credit.	
11. I don't know whether I'm doing a good job or not. She never tells me if I'm doing well or need to work harder. I sure hope she likes my work.	
12. She believed everything he said about me. She wouldn't even listen to my side, just started yelling at me.	
13. Look, we've gone over and over this. The meeting could have been over an hour ago if we hadn't gotten hung up on this one point. If we can't make a decision, let's table it and move on.	
14. Look, I know I acted like a rat. I apologized, and I'm trying to make up for it. I can't do anymore, can I? So drop it!	
15. How can I tell him how I really feel? He might get mad and then we'd start arguing. He'll think I don't love him if I tell him my real feelings.	

NAME _____

7.5   PARAPHRASING INFORMATION

❖ Activity Type: Skill Builder

PURPOSE

To help you become skillful at paraphrasing the informational aspect of a speaker's message.

INSTRUCTIONS

1. Join with three partners to create a foursome. Label the members A, B, C, and D.
2. A and B review the list below, choosing the topic upon which they disagree most widely.
3. A and B conduct a five-minute conversation on the topic they have chosen. During this period, the speakers may not express their own ideas until they have paraphrased the other person's position to his or her satisfaction. (If A and B finish discussing one item, they should move on to a second one from the list below.) C observes A; D observes B.
4. At the end of the conversation, the observers should review the listening with the persons they observed.
5. Steps 2–4 are now repeated with the roles of conversationalists and observers reversed.

TOPICS

Indicate your position on each statement below by circling one of the following labels:

TA = totally agree   A = agree   D = disagree   TD = totally disagree

1.	Despite the value of classes such as this one, in the last analysis good communicators are born, not made.	TA A D TD
2.	One measure of a person's effectiveness as a communicator is how well he or she is liked by others.	TA A D TD
3.	No matter how unreasonable or rude they are, people deserve to be treated with respect.	TA A D TD
4.	An effective communicator should be able to handle any situation in a way that leaves the other person feeling positive about the interaction.	TA A D TD

5. Interpersonal communication classes should be a required part of everyone's post-secondary education.

TA   **A**   **D**   **TD**

6. Most of what is taught in interpersonal communication classes is really common sense.

TA   **A**   **D**   **TD**

Or as an alternative

1. Choose a topic of interest to you and a partner (music, politics, religion, men, women, morals, etc.). It is best if you anticipate some difference of opinion on the topic.
2. Take turns stating your opinion. The only rule is that before you can take your turn stating *your* opinion, you must paraphrase the content of your partner's opinion *to his or her satisfaction.*

NAME _____

7.6 LISTENING AND RESPONDING STYLES

❖ Activity Type: Oral Skill

PURPOSE
To give you practice in using different listening styles to enhance listening effectiveness.

INSTRUCTIONS

1. With a partner, decide on communication situations that require effective listening. The situations should be real for the person describing them and might involve a problem, a decision that needs to be made, an issue of importance, or a change in a relationship.
2. Have your partner tell you the problem/decision/issue/relationship while you listen effectively.
3. You then tell your partner of your problem/decision/issue/relationship while your partner listens effectively.
4. Analyze the listening styles you used. Which were most/least effective in this situation? Which styles do you need to work on?
5. Use the checklist below to evaluate listening effectiveness.

CHECKLIST

5 = Superior   4 = Excellent   3 = Good   2 = Fair   1 = Poor

Uses appropriate language and nonverbal behaviours that

demonstrate genuine interest _____

seem compatible with your personal communication style _____

Uses a balance of the following types of helping responses, as appropriate _____

For both understanding and supporting

prompting _____

genuine questions _____

paraphrasing _____

concisely and clearly reflects speaker's thoughts _____

concisely and clearly reflects speaker's feelings _____

requests confirmation of paraphrase accuracy _____

For supporting only (as appropriate)

analyzing _____

advising _____

supporting (comforting, praising, agreeing, humour)   _____

Total   _____

Based on self-observation (class feedback, videotape, etc.) and personal reflection, answer the following questions.

Which listening styles did you rely on most in this situation?

_____

_____

_____

Which listening styles were most/least effective in this situation?

_____

_____

_____

Which combination of responses could you have used in this situation, and which could you use in the future to be most effective?

_____

_____

_____

NAME _____

7.7   WHAT WOULD YOU SAY? REALLY!

◆ Activity Type: Skill Builder

PURPOSE
To help you explore your typical listening-to-help responses and alternatives you might use.

INSTRUCTIONS
1. For each situation in the chart that follows, imagine that you have been approached by someone who is speaking to you about a problem that he or she has. What would you instinctively say to that person? Record your exact words. Don't worry about the "right" response. Respond in whatever way you think is most likely for you.
2. Next, review each of your responses and identify which of the different types of helpful listening responses (i.e., advising, judging, analyzing, questioning, supporting, prompting, paraphrasing) you used in each case. Record the types in the middle column of the chart.
3. Finally, look over the types of responses you identified in the middle column and determine which of the seven listening-to-help styles you did *not* use. Create new responses for each of the original situations using one of the styles not identified in the middle column. For example, if you identified that you only used advice and questions in the middle column, create new responses in the right column using either an analyzing, prompting, judging, or paraphrasing style.

SITUATION/STATEMENT	YOUR INSTINCTIVE RESPONSE	TYPES OF RESPONSE USED	NEW RESPONSE USING ANOTHER TYPE OF RESPONSE
1. I don't know what to do about things at work. We're a small staff group and we've been together for years. Right now three people are sort of ganging up on another person and being really nasty to her. Now she's talking about quitting. I just don't know what to do.			
2. I've been pretty discouraged lately. I just can't get a good relationship going with any guys – I mean a romantic relationship . . . you know. I have plenty of men that I'm good friends with, but that's always as far as it goes. I'm tired of being just a pal. I want to be more than that.			
3. Things really seem to be kind of lousy in my marriage lately. It's not that we fight too much or anything, but all the excitement seems to be gone. It's like we're in a rut, and it keeps getting worse.			
4. I keep getting the idea that my instructor's angry with me. It seems as if lately he hasn't been joking around very much, and he hasn't said anything at all about my work for about three weeks now. I wonder what I should do.			

NAME _____

7.8   MEDIATED MESSAGES—LISTENING

❖ Activity Type: Group Discussion

PURPOSE
To analyze listening behaviours in mediated contexts.

INSTRUCTIONS
Discuss each of the questions below in your group. Prepare written answers for your instructor, or be prepared to contribute to a large group discussion, comparing your experiences with those of others in your class.

1. The media influence our listening or nonlistening (e.g., the brief segments we have become accustomed to on radio and television discourage focused listening). Discuss any similar difficulties (focusing, attention span) that your group members have experienced with the listening process.

    _____

    _____

    _____

2. Describe any ineffective listening styles discussed that your group thinks are more predominant in mediated contexts.

    _____

    _____

    _____

3. What types of listening may be done more effectively through mediated channels (e.g., informational listening versus listening to help)?

    _____

    _____

    _____

4. How might you be a more effective "listener" when you use mediated channels (e.g., telephone, voice mail, e-mail, chat groups) to receive and respond to others' messages?

_____

_____

_____

NAME _____

7.9   YOUR CALL—LISTENING

❖ Activity Type: Group Discussion

PURPOSE
To evaluate the appropratness of different listening styles in a relationship.

INSTRUCTIONS
Use the case below and the discussion questions that follow to discuss the variety of communication issues involved in effective communication. Make notes on this page, add other pages on your own, or prepare a group report/analysis based on your discussion. Add your own experiences to individualize the analysis to make it "Your Call."

CASE
Arleen and Valerie have been friends since elementary school and are now in their thirties. Valerie has been happily married for 10 years. Arleen has been engaged four times and each time has broken it off as the mariage date has approached. Valerie has listened, mainly questioning, supporting, and paraphrasing. Arleen has just announced another engagement

1. Valerie wants to give Arleen advice this time. Should she? If she did, what would she say? Evaluate the possible effects on their relationship.

   _____

   _____

2. Because Valerie has known Arleen for so long, do you think she should use an analyzing style? If she did, what would she say?

   _____

   _____

3. What listening style(s) do you think would be most helpful to Arleen? What would she say in the listening style(s) you have chosen?

   _____

   _____

4. Pretend you are Valerie. Consider the situation, the other person, and yourself. Given these considerations, how would you listen? Give examples.

_____

_____

5. Suppose that the two friends described here are both men. Would your advice in any of the preceding questions change?

_____

_____

STUDY GUIDE

CROSSWORD PUZZLE

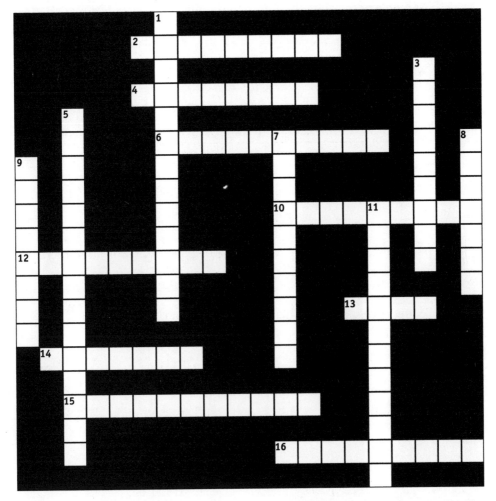

Across

2 a listening style in which the listener gives an alternative interpretation of the speaker's problem

4 a response in which the words of the speaker are repeated

6 a response style in which the receiver reassures, comforts, or distracts the person seeking help

10 using silences and brief statements of encouragement to draw out a speaker

12 a response style in which the receiver responds only to messages that interest him or her

13 a type of question that allows greater expression of the speaker's thoughts and feelings

14 the physiological dimensions of listening

15 an ineffective listening style in which the listener accepts the speaker's words at face value, resulting in failure to recognize the thoughts or feelings that are not directly expressed by the speaker

16 a response style in which the receiver perceives a speaker's comments as an attack

Down

1 occurs when sense is made of a message

3 the process of filtering out distractions when listening

5 an imitation of true listening in which the receiver's mind is elsewhere

7 giving observable feedback to the speaker

8 a reaction in which the receiver evaluates the sender's message either favourably or unfavourably

9 a helping response in which the receiver offers suggestions about how the speaker should deal with a problem

11 restating a speaker's thoughts and feelings in the listener's own words

TRUE/FALSE

Mark the statements below as true or false. Correct statements that are false on the lines below to create a true statement.

_____   **1.** Women are more likely than men to offer messages of support.

_____   **2.** Speaking is active; listening is passive.

_____   **3.** Even if they are inaccurate, paraphrases are still helpful.

_____   **4.** People should do more paraphrasing than any other style of listening.

_____   **5.** In careful listening, the heart rate quickens and respiration increases.

_____   **6.** People speak at about the same rate as others are capable of understanding their speech.

_____   **7.** The advantages of listening are more obvious to people than the advantages of speaking.

_____   **8.** Paraphrasing is the most accurate listening response you can make.

_____   **9.** Judging listening responses may be favourable or negative.

_____   **10.** Even an accurate form of analytic listening can create defensiveness because it may imply superiority and evaluativeness.

COMPLETION

Fill in the blanks below with the correct terms chosen from the list below.

residual message   shift-response   conversational narcissist
sincere question   counterfeit question   constructive criticism
attending   understanding   hearing
diversion

1. _____ is a name given to a nonlistening stage-hog.

2. _____ is a genuine request for new information aimed at understanding others.

3. _____ is the information we store (remember) after processing
information from teachers, friends, radio, TV, and other sources.

4. _____ is a type of stage-hogging strategy in which the focus of
the conversation is changed from the speaker to the stage-hog.

5. _____ is a query that is a disguised attempt to send a message,
not receive one.

6. _____ is a lesser form of negative judgment which is intended to
help the problem-holder improve in the future.

7. _____ is a listening response that helps speakers by getting their
minds off their troubles and on to something else.

8. _____ is the psychological process of listening.

9. _____ is the process of making sense of a message.

10. _____ is the physiological process of listening.

MULTIPLE CHOICE

Match the letter of the listening type with its example found below.

a. advising   c. analyzing   e. supporting   g. paraphrasing
b. judging   d. questioning   f. prompting

_____   1. "So what do you mean?"

_____   2. "You're afraid he won't come back?"

_____   3. "You're probably just more upset than usual because of the stress of
exams."

_____   4. "When did he say that?"

_____ **5.** "Well, that was good of him not to complain."

_____ **6.** "Have you tried praising her?"

_____ **7.** "Have you tried talking to him about it?"

_____ **8.** "You sound pretty confused by it all . . . is that it?"

_____ **9.** "Johan should not have said that to Aziza after you asked him not to."

_____ **10.** "And then what happened?"

_____ **11.** "So why did you go to Bakari's in the first place?"

_____ **12.** "I just want you to know that I'm here for you."

_____ **13.** "It's not fair for you to have to work nights."

_____ **14.** "If I were you, I'd do it this way."

_____ **15.** "And so you feel like retaliating because you're hurt?"

_____ **16.** "Maybe you're a little insecure because of the divorce?"

_____ **17.** "Like what?"

_____ **18.** "What makes you think that he's cheating?"

_____ **19.** "You've always earned those grades before – I know you can do it again."

_____ **20.** "No, I think you're more undecided than afraid . . ."

Choose the best informational paraphrasing response to each statement below.

21. Boss to employee: "Draft a letter that denies this request for a refund, but make it tactful."
   a. "What do you want me to say?"
   b. "How can I say no tactfully?"
   c. "So I should explain nicely why we can't give a refund, right?"
   d. "In other words, you want me to give this customer the brush-off?"

22. Friend says, "How do they expect us to satisfy the course requirements when there aren't enough spaces in the classes we're supposed to take?"
   a. "So you're frustrated because you can't get into the courses you need, huh?"
   b. "You think that some of the courses are worthless – is that it?"
   c. "Sounds like you're sorry you chose this major."
   d. "Why don't you write a letter to the chairperson of the department?"

23. Your mother says, "There's no way you're going out Friday night unless you clean up your act."
    a. "Your should clean up your act too."
    b. "Where should I start?"
    c. "You want me to start getting to school on time?"
    d. "Did you just get your hair done?"

24. Co-worker advises, "When you go in for a job interview, be sure and talk about the internship, your coursework, and your extracurricular activities. Don't expect them to ask you."
    a. "You think they won't ask about those things?"
    b. "Won't that sound like bragging?"
    c. "Why should I talk about the internship?"
    d. "So you're saying not to be bashful about stressing my experience?"

25. Friend says, "I don't think it's right that they go out and recruit women when there are plenty of good men around."
    a. "Sounds like you're angry because you think they're so concerned about being fair to women that they're being unfair to men, right?"
    b. "You're right – that doesn't sound fair."
    c. "If you don't think it's fair, you ought to speak up."
    d. "I can see that you're angry. What makes you think women are being given an unfair advantage?"

For each of the statements below, identify which response is the most complete and accurate problem-solving reflection of the speaker's thoughts and feelings.

26. "Sometimes I think I'd like to drop out of school, but then I start to feel like a quitter."
    a. "Maybe it would be helpful to take a break. You can always come back, you know."
    b. "You're afraid that you might fail if you stay in school now, is that it?"
    c. "I can really relate to what you're saying. I feel awkward here myself sometimes."
    d. "So you'd feel ashamed of yourself if you quit now, even though you'd like to?"

27. "I don't want to go to the party. I won't know anyone there, and I'll wind up sitting by myself all night."
    a. "You're afraid that you won't be able to approach anybody and nobody will want to talk to you?"
    b. "You never know; you could have a great time."
    c. "So you really don't want to go, eh?"
    d. "What makes you think it will be that way?"

28. "I get really nervous talking to my professor. I keep thinking that I sound stupid."
    a. "Talking to her is really a frightening experience?"
    b. "You're saying that you'd rather not approach her?"
    c. "You get the idea that she's evaluating you, and that leaves you feeling uncomfortable?"
    d. "You think that talking to her might affect your grade for the worse?"

29. "I'm not sure if Alec is the right guy for me . . ."

    a.   "That's it for men, eh?"

    b.   "So . . . how long have you felt this way?"

    c.   "Are you saying the wedding is off?"

    d.   "So . . . you're worried that you have more differences than commonalities – is that it?"

30. "I just blew another test in that class. Why can't I do better?"

    a.   "You probably need to study harder. You'll get it!"

    b.   "You're feeling sorry for yourself because you've done all you can do and you still can't earn a better grade?"

    c.   "Where do you think the problem is?"

    d.   "You're discouraged and frustrated because you don't know what you're doing wrong?"

STUDY GUIDE ANSWERS

CROSSWORD PUZZLE

Across:

2. analyzing
4. verbatim
6. supporting
9. adv... (a d v i n g)
10. prompting
12. elective
13. open
14. hearing
15. insensitive
16. defensive

Down:

1. u (understanding)
3. attending
5. pseudo... (p s e u d o)
7. responding
8. judging
11. paraphrasing

TRUE/FALSE

1. T	**3.** T	**5.** T	**7.** F	**9.** T
2. F	**4.** F	**6.** F	**8.** F	**10.** T

COMPLETION

1. conversational narcissist
2. sincere question
3. residual message
4. shift-response
5. counterfeit question
6. constructive criticism
7. diversion
8. attending
9. understanding
10. hearing

MULTIPLE CHOICE

1.	f	**7.**	a	**13.**	b	**19.**	e	**25.**	a
2.	g	**8.**	g	**14.**	a	**20.**	c	**26.**	d
3.	c	**9.**	b	**15.**	g	**21.**	c	**27.**	a
4.	d	**10.**	f	**16.**	c	**22.**	a	**28.**	c
5.	b	**11.**	d	**17.**	f	**23.**	c	**29.**	d
6.	a	**12.**	e	**18.**	d	**24.**	d	**30.**	d

CHAPTER 8

Communication and Relational Dynamics

OUTLINE
Use this outline to take notes as you read the chapter in the text and/or as your instructor lectures in class.

I. **Why we form relationships**

    A. **Attraction**
        1. Similarity and complementarity
        2. Reciprocal attraction
        3. Competence
        4. Disclosure
        5. Proximity

    B. **Intimacy**
        1. The dimensions of intimacy
           a. Physical
           b. Intellectual
           c. Emotional
           d. Shared activities
        2. Masculine and feminine intimacy styles
           a. Self-disclosure
           b. Shared activities
        3. Cultural influences on intimacy
           a. Historical
           b. Cultural
               1) Class/group
               2) Collectivist
               3) Individualist
        4. The limits of intimacy

    C. **Rewards, Costs, and Outcomes—Social Exchange Theory**

II.   Models of relational development and maintenance

A. **Developmental Models**
   1. Initiating
   2. Experimenting
   3. Intensifying
   4. Integrating
   5. Bonding
   6. Differentiating
   7. Circumscribing
   8. Stagnating
   9. Avoiding
   10. Terminating

B. **Dialectical Perspectives**
   1. Dialectical tensions
      a. Connection vs. autonomy
      b. Predictability vs. novelty
      c. Openness vs. privacy
   2. Strategies for managing dialectical tensions
      a. Denial
      b. Disorientation
      c. Alternation
      d. Balance
      e. Integration
      f. Recalibration
      g. Reaffirmation

C. **Chracteristics of Relational Development and Maintenance**
   1. Relationships are constantly changing
   2. Movement is always to a new place

III.   Self-disclosure in relationships

A. **Definition**
   1. Deliberate
   2. Significant
   3. Not known by others

B. **Degrees of Self-Disclosure**
   1. Social penetration model: Breadth and depth
   2. Types: Clichés, facts, opinions, feelings

C. **A Model of Self-Disclosure: Open, Hidden, Blind, Unknown**

D. **Characteristics of Self-Disclosure**
   1. Usually occurs in dyads
   2. Occurs incrementally
   3. Few transactions involve high levels
   4. Relatively scarce
   5. Usually occurs in positive relationships

E. **Reasons for Self-Disclosure**
1. Catharsis
2. Self-clarification
3. Self-validation
4. Reciprocity
5. Identity management
6. Relationship maintenance and enhancement
7. Social control
8. Manipulation

F. **Guidelines for Self-Disclosure**
1. Consider the importance of the other person
2. Evaluate the risks involved
3. Make the disclosure relevant to the situation at hand
4. Make the amount and type of self-disclosure appropriate
5. Consider constructive effects
6. Make the disclosure clear and understandable
7. Reciprocate disclosure as appropriate

IV. Alternatives to self-disclosure

A. **Lying**
1. White lies
2. Reasons for lying
   a. Save face
   b. Avoid tension/conflict
   c. Guide social interaction
   d. Expand/reduce relationships
   e. Gain power
3. Effects of lies – threats to the relationship

B. **Equivocal Language**
1. Spares embarrassment
2. Saves face
3. Saves speaker from being caught lying

C. **Hinting**
1. Saves receiver from embarrassment
2. Saves sender from embarrassment

D. **The Ethics of Evasion**

KEY TERMS

Use these key terms to review major concepts from your text. Write the definition for each key term in the space to the right.

alternation _____

attraction _____

avoiding _____

balance _____

bonding _____

breadth _____

catharsis _____

circumscribing _____

clichés _____

connection–autonomy dialectic _____

denial _____

depth _____

dialectical tensions _____

differentiating _____

disorientation _____

emotional intimacy _____

equivocal language _____

experimenting _____

facts _____

feelings _____

hinting _____

identity management _____

initiating _____

integrating _____

intellectual intimacy _____

intensifying _____

intimacy _____

Johari Window _____

lying _____

manipulation _____

openness–privacy dialectic _____

opinions _____

physical intimacy _____

predictability–novelty dialectic _____

proximity _____

reaffirmation _____

recalibration _____

reciprocal attraction _____

reciprocity _____

relational enhancement _____

relational maintenance _____

rewards _____

self-clarification _____

self-disclosure _____

self-validation _____

similarity _____

small talk _____

social control _____

social exchange theory _____

social penetration _____

stages of relationships _____

stagnating _____

terminating _____

uncertainty reduction _____

white lie _____

NAME _____

ACTIVITIES

8.1 DISCOVERING DIALECTICS

◆ Activity Type: Invitation to Insight

PURPOSE
To identify and describe behaviours that contribute to dialectical tensions in relationships.

INSTRUCTIONS
1. Identify the dialectical tensions operating in the following situations, taking time to explain the conflicting feelings and thoughts in each.
2. Identify one or more of the seven strategies for managing dialectical tensions (denial, disorientation, balance, alternation, integration, recalibration, and reaffirmation) that you believe would be most beneficial to the relationship, and explain how the relationship would deal with the dialectical tension under these circumstances.
3. Next describe dialectical tensions at work in your own relationships and label and explain the strategies that you use to deal with them.

SITUATION	DIALECTICAL TENSION	STRATEGY FOR MANAGING
EXAMPLE Thalia, 19, and her mother, Agnes, have become good friends over the past few years. Thalia now has a serious boyfriend and spends less time talking to her mother.	The openness–privacy dialectic is probably at work here. Thalia and Agnes continue to share the intimacy of their mother–daughter relationship, but privacy needs about the boyfriend probably keep them at greater distance.	Thalia and Agnes are likely to use the balance strategy, in which they maintain openness about many areas, but keep certain parts of the boyfriend relationship "off limits."

SITUATION	DIALECTICAL TENSION	STRATEGY FOR MANAGING
1. Spiros is new to the software firm where Steve has been for five years. Spiros has asked Steve to play golf this weekend. Steve is uncomfortable about mixing business and pleasure, but still wants to have a good working relationship with Spiros.		
2. Nesto and Gina have been dating for six months. They continue to enjoy each other's company, but both of them have begun to notice annoying little habits that the other one has.		
3. Alger and Barnard are siblings who have always relied on each other completely. Alger appreciates Barnard's dependability, but wishes their relationship weren't so boring.		
4. Eugenia and Shane have worked at the same business for 20 years. They have collaborated on a number of projects. They've tried to get together socially, but Eugenia's husband and Shane's wife don't seem to get along.		

SITUATION	DIALECTICAL TENSION	STRATEGY FOR MANAGING
5. Christina and Nicole are roommates. Christina wants them to share everything, but Nicole is not proud of a few things she's done and doesn't want to face her friend's judgment.		
6.		
7.		
8.		

NAME _____

8.2   BREADTH AND DEPTH OF RELATIONSHIPS

◆ Activity Type: Invitation to Insight

PURPOSES

1. To help you understand the breadth and depth of a relationship that is important to you.
2. To help you decide if you are satisfied with the breadth and depth of that relationship, and possibly to modify it.

INSTRUCTIONS

1. Use the form below to make a social penetration model for a significant relationship you have, indicating the depth and breadth of various areas. See Figures 8.5 and 8.6 in Chapter 8 of *Looking Out/Looking In* for examples of the social penetration model.
2. Answer the questions at the end of the exercise.

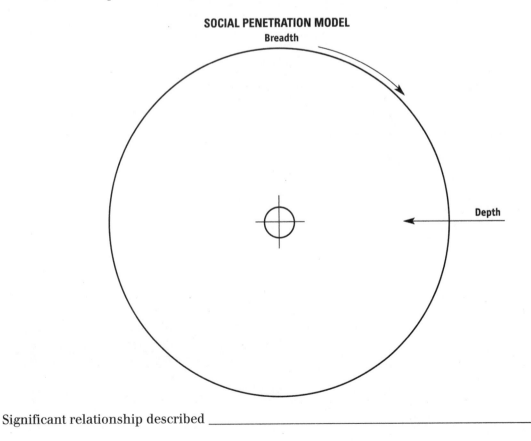

SOCIAL PENETRATION MODEL

Significant relationship described _____

CONCLUSIONS

How deep or shallow is your relationship with this person?

_____

_____

Does the depth vary from one area (breadth) to another? In what way?

_____

_____

_____

Are you satisfied with the depth and breadth of this relationship?

_____

_____

_____

What could you do to change the relationship?

_____

_____

_____

_____

_____

_____

_____

_____

NAME _____

8.3 REASONS FOR NONDISCLOSURE*

◆ Activity Type: Invitation to Insight

PURPOSE
To give you an idea of the reasons you do not disclose and the rationality of these reasons.

INSTRUCTIONS
1. Choose a particular individual about whom you want to analyze your self-disclosing behaviour.
2. In the column to the left of each item, indicate the extent to which you use each reason to avoid disclosing.

   5 = almost always   2 = rarely
   4 = often   1 = never
   3 = sometimes

3. In the column to the right of each item, indicate how reasonable and realistic the reason is.
   5 = totally realistic
   4 = mostly realistic
   3 = partly realistic, partly unrealistic
   2 = mostly unrealistic
   1 = totally unrealistic

HOW FREQUENTLY DO YOU USE THE REASON?		HOW REALISTIC AND RATIONAL IS THE REASON?
_____	1. I can't find the opportunity to self-disclose with this person.	_____
_____	2. If I disclose I might hurt the other person.	_____
_____	3. If I disclose I might be evaluating or judging the person.	_____
_____	4. I can't think of topics that I would disclose.	_____
_____	5. Self-disclosure would give information that might be used against me at some time.	_____
_____	6. If I disclose it might cause me to make personal changes.	_____

---

*Based on a survey developed by Lawrence B. Rosenfeld, "Self-Disclosure Avoidance: Why Am I Afraid to Tell You Who I Am?" *Communication Monographs* 46 (1979): 63–74.

HOW FREQUENTLY DO YOU USE THE REASON?		**HOW REALISTIC AND RATIONAL IS THE REASON?**
_____	7. Self-disclosure might threaten relationships I have with people other than the close acquaintance to whom I disclose.	_____
_____	8. Self-disclosure is a sign of weakness.	_____
_____	9. If I disclose I might lose control over the other person.	_____
_____	10. If I disclose I might discover I am less than I wish to be.	_____
_____	11. If I disclose I might project an image I do not want to project.	_____
_____	12. If I disclose the other person might not understand what I was saying.	_____
_____	13. If I disclose the other person might evaluate me negatively.	_____
_____	14. Self-disclosure is a sign of some emotional disturbance.	_____
_____	15. Self-disclosure might hurt our relationship.	_____
_____	16. I am afraid that self-disclosure might lead to an intimate relationship with the other person.	_____
_____	17. Self-disclosure might threaten my physical safety.	_____
_____	18. If I disclose I might give information that makes me appear inconsistent.	_____
_____	19. Any other reasons: _____	_____

What does this personal survey tell you about your thoughts and feelings about self-disclosure with this person?

_____

_____

_____

Do you think your level of self-disclosure is appropriate or inappropriate with this person? Why?

_____

_____

_____

NAME _____

8.4 DEGREES OF SELF-DISCLOSURE

◆ Activity Type: Invitation to Insight

PURPOSES

1. To demonstrate that self-disclosure can operate on a variety of levels, some quite intimate and others less revealing.
2. To give you practice in applying various types of self-disclosure to personal situations.

INSTRUCTIONS

For each of the following topics, write two statements for each level of self-disclosure. (See Chapter 8 of *Looking Out/Looking In* for descriptions of each level.)

EXAMPLE

TOPIC: SCHOOL

1. Clichés
    a. *These exams sure are a drag!*
    b. *Textbooks sure are expensive!*

2. Facts
    a. *I'm a psychology major at the University of Ottawa.*
    b. *I'm getting a teaching certificate so I'll be able to teach social studies.*

3. Opinions
    a. *I believe in employment equity but I don't think there should be quotas for women and minorities.*
    b. *I don't think instructors should count class participation as part of a person's grade.*

4. Feelings
    a. *I feel scared when I think about the future. I'm almost finished with three years of college, and I'm still confused about what to do with my life.*
    b. *I get angry when Professor Autel doesn't prepare for our class.*

TOPIC: MY FAMILY

1. Clichés

    a. _____

    b. _____

2. Facts

a. _____

b. _____

3. Opinions

a. _____

b. _____

4. Feelings

a. _____

b. _____

TOPIC: MY CAREER PLANS

1. Clichés

a. _____

b. _____

2. Facts

a. _____

b. _____

3. Opinions

a. _____

b. _____

4. Feelings

a. _____

b. _____

TOPIC: MY FRIENDSHIPS

1. Clichés

    a. _____

    b. _____

2. Facts

    a. _____

    b. _____

3. Opinions

    a. _____

    b. _____

4. Feelings

    a. _____

    b. _____

TOPIC: SPORTS

1. Clichés

    a. _____

    b. _____

2. Facts

    a. _____

    b. _____

3. Opinions

    a. _____

    b. _____

4. Feelings

    a. _____

    b. _____

NAME _____

8.5 RESPONSES IN RELATIONSHIPS

❖ Activity Type: Skill Builder

PURPOSES
1. To generate responses to relational situations.
2. To evaluate the effectiveness and ethics of each situation.

INSTRUCTIONS
1. In groups, use the situations described below to record your possible words for each type of response listed.
2. Evaluate the effectiveness and ethics of your response.
3. Record an example of a situation of your own.

EXAMPLE

Your friend asks you if you had a good time when you went out with his cousin last night.

Self-disclosure *I didn't have a great time, but then we were just getting to know one another. I don't think we had much in common.*
Partial disclosure *I had fun when we went to the movie.*
White lie or lie *Your cousin was a lot of fun and the movie was great.*
Hinting or equivocation *First dates are really times of discovery, aren't they?*
Which response is most effective/which most ethical? *I think the white lie was the most effective here. While I wasn't exactly truthful with my friend, I just don't want to tell him how boring I think his cousin is. I think it is better just to be nice to him and his cousin. Then both of them can save face, too.*

1. A family member calls and asks how you are doing in classes.

   Self-disclosure _____

   _____

   Partial disclosure _____

   _____

   White lie or lie _____

   _____

   Hinting or equivocation _____

   _____

Which response is most effective/which most ethical? _____

_____

_____

2. You are applying to rent an apartment that prohibits pets. You have a cat.

Self-disclosure _____

_____

Partial disclosure _____

_____

White lie or lie _____

_____

Hinting or equivocation _____

_____

Which response is most effective/which most ethical? _____

_____

_____

3. You are being interviewed by a group of people to rent a room in the house they
    live in. They want to know if you are loud, clean, responsible, and the like.

Self-disclosure _____

_____

Partial disclosure _____

_____

White lie or lie _____

_____

Hinting or equivocation _____

_____

Which response is most effective/which most ethical? _____

_____

_____

4. Your roommates ask what you think of the bright posters they've just put up around the room.

Self-disclosure _____

_____

Partial disclosure _____

_____

White lie or lie _____

_____

Hinting or equivocation _____

_____

Which response is most effective/which most ethical? _____

_____

_____

5. Your romantic partner asks how many other people you've really loved before you met him or her.

Self-disclosure _____

_____

Partial disclosure _____

_____

White lie or lie _____

_____

Hinting or equivocation _____

_____

Which response is most effective/which most ethical? _____

_____

_____

6. Your instuctor casually asks you what you do for relaxation and fun.

Self-disclosure _____

_____

Partial disclosure _____

_____

White lie or lie _____

_____

Hinting or equivocation _____

_____

Which response is most effective/which most ethical? _____

_____

_____

7. Your boss at work wants to know what your plans for the future are.

Self-disclosure _____

_____

Partial disclosure _____

_____

White lie or lie _____

_____

Hinting or equivocation _____

_____

Which response is most effective/which most ethical? _____

_____

_____

8. Your mother asks you what your brother/sister has been up to lately.

Self-disclosure _____

_____

Partial disclosure _____

_____

White lie or lie _____

_____

Hinting or equivocation _____

_____

Which response is most effective/which most ethical? _____

_____

_____

9. Your romantic partner wants to know why you are spending so much time with your other friends.

Self-disclosure _____

_____

Partial disclosure _____

_____

White lie or lie _____

_____

Hinting or equivocation _____

_____

Which response is most effective/which most ethical? _____

_____

_____

Record an example of your own here.

10. _____

_____

Self-disclosure _____

_____

Partial disclosure _____

_____

White lie or lie _____

_____

Hinting or equivocation _____

_____

Which response is most effective/which most ethical? _____

_____

_____

NAME _____

8.6   RELATIONAL STAGES AND SELF-DISCLOSURE

❖ Activity Type: Skill Builder

PURPOSES
1. To analyze different degrees of self-disclosure.
2. To discuss the appropriate levels of self-disclosure for different relational stages.

INSTRUCTIONS
1. In a group, discuss the various situations listed below.
2. Identify the types of responses that will be likely (equivocation, lies, hinting, disclosure – include the level, such as fact or feeling).
3. Determine the function that response serves in the relationship.
4. Identify the relational stage that may be illustrated by this type of response.

EXAMPLE

Two friends are discussing the effects of divorce in their families.

Type(s) of responses likely *Self-disclosure is likely to occur in this situation. Because they have similar experiences, the likelihood of reciprocity of self-disclosure is high. It will probably come from the highest levels of self-disclosure, feelings, but might also include a number of facts.*
Function in relationship *The self-disclosure functions to maintain the relationship, to increase intellectual and emotional intimacy, and to advance the stage of the relationship.*
Relational stage illustrated *This type of self-disclosure would most likely occur in an intensifying stage of a relationship, where the friends have gone beyond the small talk of experimenting and are beginning to develop more trust, more depth rather than breadth of self-disclosure, and where secrets are told and favours given.*

1. Friends are telling one another about their use of/refusal to use drugs.

   Type(s) of responses likely _____

   _____

   Function in relationship _____

   _____

   Relational stage illustrated _____

   _____

2. Two classmates are comparing their grades.

Type(s) of responses likely _____

_____

Function in relationship _____

_____

Relational stage illustrated _____

_____

3. A boyfriend and girlfriend are telling one another about their past romantic involvements.

Type(s) of responses likely _____

_____

Function in relationship _____

_____

Relational stage illustrated _____

_____

4. Two friends are shopping for clothes and giving one another advice on what looks good/bad.

Type(s) of responses likely _____

_____

Function in relationship _____

_____

Relational stage illustrated _____

_____

5. A parent asks a 20-year-old about his or her weekend.

Type(s) of responses likely _____

_____

Function in relationship _____

_____

Relational stage illustrated _____

_____

6. A manager and employee have agreed to sit down and talk about the problems they are experiencing with each other.

Type(s) of responses likely _____

_____

Function in relationship _____

_____

Relational stage illustrated _____

_____

7. A friend has just experienced a death in the family and the partner is expressing concern.

Type(s) of responses likely _____

_____

Function in relationship _____

_____

Relational stage illustrated _____

_____

8. Two friends are exchanging information about the state of their marriages.

Type(s) of responses likely _____

_____

Function in relationship _____

_____

Relational stage illustrated _____

_____

9. Two women are discussing childbearing.

Type(s) of responses likely _____

_____

Function in relationship _____

_____

Relational stage illustrated _____

_____

10. Two friends are discussing their worries and feelings of responsibility regarding their parents' advancing age.

Type(s) of responses likely _____

_____

Function in relationship _____

_____

Relational stage illustrated _____

_____

NAME _____

8.7   THE INTERVIEW

❖ Activity Type: Invitation to Insight

PURPOSE

To practise participating in low-level disclosure and get to know another person better as a result.

BACKGROUND

"Low-level" disclosure means that you will be asking and will be asked for only facts or opinions. You share only what you wish to. The questions will leave a lot of room for personal choice in terms of how to respond. It's possible that you may choose to risk sharing high-level disclosures in your responses, but you may choose not to. More interesting than what you disclose is perhaps your reasons for choosing that level.

INSTRUCTIONS

1. Partner with a classmate. If possible, choose someone you haven't been able to spend as much time with as with others.
2. Each partner takes a turn interviewing the other.
3. Conduct each interview by asking any five of the questions in the following list. You may also want to open the interview up to other questions that occur to you. Each partner can select different questions to ask.
4. Then with your partner, discuss anything you learned about the other person as well as how it felt to disclose in this kind of situation. Did any of the questions cause discomfort? How did you handle that? How much time did you spend thinking about breadth and depth before disclosing? Was it a consideration?

INTERVIEW QUESTIONS

What is difficult for you to do?
What's very easy for you to do?
When do you feel most comfortable?
When do you feel uncomfortable?
If you weren't in your chosen field of study or work, what would you most like to be doing?
How do you deal with your own anger?
How do you respond to other people's anger?
Where do you go to get in touch with yourself? How do you do that?
What's a dream you have had more than once?
Whom do you trust the most? Why?
What kinds of situations leave you feeling vulnerable or unprotected?
What would your worst enemy say about you?

What would your best friend say about you?
When people first meet you, what do you think their first impression usually is?
What's something you really wish you could learn how to do?
If reincarnation does exist, what would you like to come back as?
What's the greatest amount of physical pain you have ever endured?
What's the best birthday you have ever had? The worst?

NAME _____

8.8   MEDIATED MESSAGES—RELATIONAL DYNAMICS

❖ Activity Type: Group Discussion

PURPOSE
To analyze relational dynamics in mediated contexts.

INSTRUCTIONS
Discuss each of the questions below in your group. Prepare written answers for your instructor, or be prepared to contribute to a large group discussion, comparing your experiences with those of others in your class.

1. Identify how mediated forms of communication (e.g., instant messaging/chat, e-mail) can help us form relationships. Do mediated forms of communication make it easier to form relationships, or are we more isolated relationally because of mediated communication?

_____

_____

2. When people are physically separated, maintaining relationships is difficult. Discuss how mediated forms of communication might be employed effectively in these cases. Can satisfying relationships be maintained without face-to-face communication?

_____

_____

3. Self-disclosure is important to the development of relationships. Describe how self-disclosure might occur differently in mediated contexts (letters, e-mail, telephone, instant messaging/chat, online courses) than in fact-to-face communication.

_____

_____

4. Intimacy is an important aspect of relationships. Discuss how physical, intellectual, and emotional intimacy (and even shared activities) can be fostered using mediated forms of communication.

_____

_____

NAME _____

8.9   YOUR CALL—RELATIONAL DYNAMICS

❖ Activity Type: Group Discussion

PURPOSE
To analyze the role of self-disclosure in a relationship.

INSTRUCTIONS
Use the case below and the discussion questions that follow to discuss the variety of communication issues involved in effective communication. Make notes on this page, add other pages on your own, or prepare a group report/analysis based on your discussion. Add your own experiences to individualize the analysis to make it "Your Call."

CASE
Leilani and Malcolm dated one another exclusively for three years. They broke up for six months and now are back together and talking about getting married. While they were apart, Leilani became intimate with a casual friend of Malcolm's for a brief time before she realized that she really loved only Malcolm. During this same time, Malcolm dated around; he was attracted to a number of women, but he did not get serious about any one. Malcolm has now told Leilani that he believes they should tell one another everything about the time they were apart.

1. Do you think full self-disclosure is important in this relationship? Why or why not?

   _____

   _____

2. Use other relationships (your own and those of others) to evaluate how important full self-disclosure is to committed relationships. Are there times when full disclosure is more harmful than helpful?

   _____

   _____

3. Evaluate the alternatives to self-disclosure in this situation. Would lies, white lies, partial disclosure, equivocation, or hinting be more effective than full disclosure? What about the short-term versus long-term effects of each alternative?

_____

_____

4. Use the guidelines for self-disclosure in *Looking Out/Looking In* to evaluate how Leilani and Malcolm should each disclose/not disclose to each other about the six months they were apart.

_____

_____

STUDY GUIDE

CROSSWORD PUZZLE

Across

1   a motivation for self-disclosing based on the research evidence that individuals disclosing information about themselves encourage others to self-disclose in return

3   tensions that exist when two opposing or incompatible forces exist simultaneously in a relationship

8   first dimension of self-disclosure involving the range of subjects being discussed

11 speech that focuses on building beginning relationships, usually focusing on similarities with the other person

13 disclosing in order to get something off your chest

15 the relationship stage in which exclusivity is declared

16 confirmation of a belief you hold about yourself

Down

2   a ritualized, stock statement delivered in response to a social situation

4   ambiguous language that has two or more equally plausible meanings

5   a state of personal sharing arising from physical, intellectual, or emotional contact

6   a deliberate attempt to hide or misrepresent the truth

7   a model that describes relationships in terms of their breadth and depth

9   a semi-economic theory of relationships that suggests we often seek out people who can give us rewards greater than or equal to the costs we encounter

10 a dimension of self-disclosure involving a shift from relatively nonrevealing messages to more personal ones

12 a way of managing dialectical challenges by avoiding difficulties

14 if these are too big, we may decide the relationship isn't worth it

MATCHING

Match the terms in column 1 with their definitions in column 2.

_____ **1.** breadth

_____ **2.** cliché

_____ **3.** depth

_____ **4.** dialectical tension

_____ **5.** equivocal language

_____ **6.** exchange theory

_____ **7.** identity management

_____ **8.** intimacy

_____ **9.** Johari Window

_____ **10.** lie

_____ **11.** manipulation

_____ **12.** reciprocity

_____ **13.** relational enhancement

_____ **14.** self-disclosure

_____ **15.** self-validation

_____ **16.** small talk

_____ **17.** social penetration

_____ **18.** staircase model

_____ **19.** uncertainty reduction

_____ **20.** white lie

a. the state that exists when two opposing or incompatible forces exist simultaneously

b. a semi-economic model of relationships that suggests that we often seek out people who can give us rewards that are greater than or equal to the costs we encounter in dealing with them

c. a model that describes relationships in terms of their breadth and depth

d. first dimension of self-disclosure involving the range of subjects being discussed

e. a model of relationships that describes broad phases of "coming together" and "coming apart"

f. speech that focuses on building beginning relationships, usually focusing on similarities with the other person

g. a deliberate attempt to hide or misrepresent the truth

h. a ritualized, stock statement delivered in response to a social situation

i. the process of getting to know others by gaining more information about them

j. a model that describes the relationship between self-disclosure and self-awareness

k. a dimension of self-disclosure involving a shift from relatively nonrevealing messages to more revealing ones

l. a motivation for self-disclosing based on creating relational success by increasing honesty and depth of sharing

m. ambiguous language that has two or more equally plausible meanings

n. a deliberate hiding or misrepresentation of the truth, intended to help, or not to harm, the receiver

o. confirmation of a belief you hold about yourself

p. a motivation for self-disclosing based on research evidence that individuals disclosing information about themselves encourage others to self-disclose in return

q. the process of deliberately revealing information about oneself that is significant and that would not normally be known by others

r. an act of self-disclosure calculated in advance to achieve a desired result

s. a state of personal sharing arising from physical, intellectual, or emotional contact

t. a relational process of revealing personal information to make ourselves more attractive

TRUE/FALSE

Mark the statements below as true or false. Correct statements that are false on the lines below to create a true statement.

_____ 1. Intimacy is definitely rewarding, so maximizing intimacy is the best way of relating to others.

_____

_____

_____ 2. Deeper disclosures are more likely in dyads.

_____

_____

_____ 3. Research shows that male–male relationships involve less disclosure than male–female or female–female relationships.

_____

_____

_____ 4. The amount of disclosure in a relationship is determined by the most open person.

_____

_____

_____   **5.** Appropriate self-disclosure is appealing in others because it's a sign of trust.

_____

_____

_____   **6.** The struggle to achieve important but seemingly incompatible goals in relationships results in the creation of dialectical tension.

_____

_____

_____   **7.** The struggle between independence and dependence in a relationship is called the openness–privacy dialectic.

_____

_____

_____   **8.** Intimacy is not the only goal of relationships.

_____

_____

_____   **9.** Research indicates that partners in intimate relationships engage in high levels of self-disclosure frequently.

_____

_____

_____   **10.** People justify over half of their lies as ways to avoid embarrassment for themselves or others.

_____

_____

COMPLETION

Fill in the blanks below with the correct terms chosen from the list below.

| open | hidden | blind | unknown | intellectual |
| integration | emotional | recalibration | hinting | balance |

1. _____ is the type of intimacy that comes from an exchange of important ideas.

2. _____ occurs when communicators change their view of a dialectical tension by reframing the apparent contradiction.

3. _____ is the type of intimacy that comes from exchanging important feelings.

4. _____ is one way to remove dialectical tension, by using compromise.

5. _____ is an acceptance of dialectical tensions without trying to diminish them.

6. _____ is a frame of the Johari Window that consists of information that you know about yourself but aren't willing to reveal to others.

7. _____ is a frame of the Johari Window that consists of information of which neither you nor the other person is aware.

8. _____ is a frame of the Johari Window that consists of information of which both you and the other person are aware.

9. _____ is a frame of the Johari Window that consists of information of which you are unaware but of which the other person is aware.

10. _____ is an alternative to self-disclosure in which the person gives only a clue to the direct meaning of the response.

MULTIPLE CHOICE

Place the letter of the developmental stage of the intimate relationship on the line before its example found below.

a. initiating
b. experimenting
c. intensifying
d. integrating
e. bonding

f. differentiating
g. circumscribing
h. stagnating
i. avoiding
j. terminating

_____ **1.** Partners begin to take on each other's commitments at this stage.

_____ **2.** First glances and sizing each other up typify this stage.

_____ **3.** Called the "we" stage, this stage involves increasing self-disclosure.

_____ **4.** Lots of "small talk" typifies this stage.

_____ **5.** This stage involves much focus on individual rather than dyadic interests.

_____ **6.** There's very little growth or experimentation in this stage.

_____ **7.** This stage involves withdrawal from issues and low energy.

_____ **8.** The partners' social circles merge at this stage.

_____ **9.** Partners start to find excuses for why they can't spend more time together at this stage.

_____ **10.** The relationship is redefined or dissolved at this stage.

_____ **11.** A marriage ceremony would be typical here.

_____ **12.** Roommates who make sure they are never in the same room and who are tolerating one another only until the lease is up might be at this stage.

_____ **13.** Two people who avoid discussing future commitment because the are afraid of how the discussion will go are probably at this stage.

_____ **14.** This stage represents most communication at a social gathering where people are just getting to know one another.

_____ **15.** In this stage, people spend an increasing amount of time together, asking for support from one another and doing favours for one another.

STUDY GUIDE ANSWERS

CROSSWORD PUZZLE

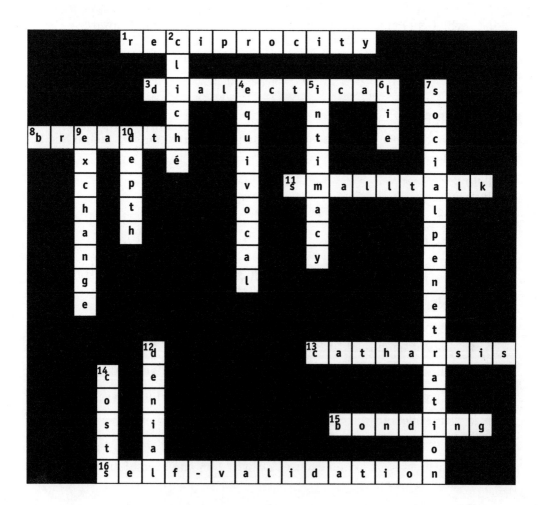

MATCHING

1. d	**5.** m	**9.** j	**13.** l	**17.** c
2. h	**6.** b	**10.** g	**14.** q	**18.** e
3. k	**7.** t	**11.** r	**15.** o	**19.** i
4. a	**8.** s	**12.** p	**16.** f	**20.** n

TRUE/FALSE

1. F	**3.** T	**5.** T	**7.** F	**9.** F
2. T	**4.** F	**6.** T	**8.** T	**10.** T

COMPLETION

1. intellectual	**5.** integration	**9.** blind
2. recalibration	**6.** hidden	**10.** hinting
3. emotional	**7.** unknown	
4. balance	**8.** open	

MULTIPLE CHOICE

1. d	**4.** b	**7.** g	**10.** j	**13.** g
2. a	**5.** f	**8.** d	**11.** e	**14.** b
3. c	**6.** h	**9.** i	**12.** i	**15.** c

CHAPTER 9

Improving Communication Climates

OUTLINE

Use this outline to take notes as you read the chapter in the text and/or as your instructor lectures in class.

I. Communication climate: The key to positive relationships

    A. Confirming Communication
1. Recognition
2. Acknowledgment
3. Endorsement

    B. Disconfirming Communication
1. Verbal abuse
2. Complaining
3. Impervious responses
4. Interrupting
5. Irrelevant responses
6. Tangential responses
7. Impersonal responses
8. Ambiguous responses
9. Incongruous responses

    C. How Communication Climates Develop
1. Escalatory conflict spirals
2. De-escalatory conflict spirals

II. Defensiveness: Causes and remedies

    A. Causes: Face-Threatening Acts

    B. Types of Defensive Reactions
1. Attacking the critic
    a. Verbal aggression
    b. Sarcasm

2. Distorting critical information
   a. Rationalization
   b. Compensation
   c. Regression
3. Avoiding dissonant information
   a. Physical avoidance
   b. Repression
   c. Apathy
   d. Displacement

C. **Preventing Defensiveness in Others**
   1. Evaluation versus description
   2. Control versus problem orientation
   3. Strategy versus spontaneity
   4. Neutrality versus empathy
   5. Superiority versus equality
   6. Certainty versus provisionalism

D. **Responding Nondefensively to Criticism**
   1. Seek more information
      a. Ask for specifics
      b. Guess about specifics
      c. Paraphrase the speaker's ideas
      d. Ask what the critic wants
      e. Ask what else is wrong
   2. Agree with the critic
      a. Agree with the facts
      b. Agree with the critic's perception

KEY TERMS

Use these key terms to review major concepts from your text. Write the definition for each key term in the space to the right.

acknowledgment _____

ambiguous response _____

apathy _____

certainty _____

cognitive dissonance _____

communication climate _____

compensation _____

complaining _____

confirming communication _____

controlling communication _____

de-escalatory conflict spiral _____

defence mechanism _____

defensiveness _____

descriptive communication _____

disconfirming communication _____

displacement _____

empathy _____

endorsement _____

equality _____

escalatory conflict spiral _____

evaluative communication _____

face-threatening act _____

Gibb categories _____

impersonal response _____

impervious response _____

incongruous response _____

interrupting _____

irrelevant response _____

neutrality _____

physical avoidance _____

problem orientation _____

provisionalism _____

rationalization _____

recognition _____

regression _____

repression _____

sarcasm _____

spiral _____

spontaneity _____

strategy _____

superiority _____

tangential response _____

verbal abuse _____

verbal aggression _____

NAME _____

ACTIVITIES

9.1   UNDERSTANDING YOUR DEFENSIVE RESPONSES

◆ Activity Type: Invitation to Insight

PURPOSE
To help you identify your typical defensive responses.

INSTRUCTIONS
1. Identify the person or people who would be most likely to deliver each of the following critical messages to you. If you are unlikely to hear one or more of the following messages, substitute a defensiveness-arousing topic of your own.
2. For each situation, describe

   a.   the person likely to deliver the message.
   b.   the typical content of the message.
   c.   the general type(s) of response you make: attacking, distorting, or avoiding.
   d.   your typical verbal response(s).
   e.   your typical nonverbal response(s).
   f.   the part(s) of your presenting self being defended.
   g.   the probable consequences of these response(s).

EXAMPLE

A negative comment about your use of time.

Person likely to deliver this message   _my parents_
Typical content of the message   _wasting my time watching TV instead of studying_
General type(s) of response   _attacking, distorting_
Your typical verbal response(s)   _"Get off my back! I work hard! I need time to relax." "I'll study later; I've got plenty of time."_
Your typical nonverbal response(s)   _harsh tone of voice, sullen silence for an hour or two_
Part(s) of presenting self being defended   _good student, not lazy_
Probable consequences of your response(s)   _uncomfortable silence, more criticism from parents in the future_

1. Negative comment about your appearance.

   Person likely to deliver this message   _____

Typical content of the message _____

_____

General type(s) of response _____

Your typical verbal response(s) _____

_____

Your typical nonverbal response(s) _____

_____

Part(s) of presenting self being defended _____

Probable consequences of your response(s) _____

_____

_____

2. Criticism about your choice of friends.

Person likely to deliver this message _____

Typical content of the message _____

_____

General type(s) of response _____

Your typical verbal response(s) _____

_____

Your typical nonverbal response(s) _____

_____

Part(s) of presenting self being defended _____

Probable consequences of your response(s) _____

_____

_____

3. Criticism of a job you've just completed.

Person likely to deliver this message _____

Typical content of the message _____

_____

General type(s) of response _____

Your typical verbal response(s) _____

_____

Your typical nonverbal response(s) _____

_____

Part(s) of presenting self being defended _____

Probable consequences of your response(s) _____

_____

_____

4. Criticism of your schoolwork.

Person likely to deliver this message _____

Typical content of the message _____

_____

General type(s) of response _____

Your typical verbal response(s) _____

_____

Your typical nonverbal response(s) _____

_____

Part(s) of presenting self being defended _____

Probable consequences of your response(s) _____

_____

_____

5. Criticism of your diet or eating habits.

Person likely to deliver this message _____

Typical content of the message _____

_____

General type(s) of response _____

Your typical verbal response(s) _____

_____

Your typical nonverbal response(s) _____

_____

Part(s) of presenting self being defended _____

Probable consequences of your response(s) _____

_____

_____

6. A negative comment about your exercise (or lack of it).

Person likely to deliver this message _____

Typical content of the message _____

_____

General type(s) of response _____

Your typical verbal response(s) _____

_____

Your typical nonverbal response(s) _____

_____

Part(s) of presenting self being defended _____

Probable consequences of your response(s) _____

_____

_____

NAME _____

9.2   DEFENSIVE AND SUPPORTIVE LANGUAGE

◆❖ Activity Type: Skill Builder

PURPOSE

To help you recognize the difference between the Gibb categories of defensive and supportive language.

INSTRUCTIONS

1. For each of the situations below, write two statements a speaker might make. One should contain evaluative language and the other descriptive language.
2. In the space adjacent to each statement, label the Gibb categories of language that your words represent.

EXAMPLE

A neighbour's late-night stereo music playing is disrupting your sleep.

Defense-arousing statement *Why don't you show a little consideration and turn that damn thing down? If I hear any more noise I'm going to call the police!*
Type(s) of defensive language *evaluation, control*
Supportive statement *When I hear your stereo music late at night I can't sleep, which leaves me more and more tired. I'd like to figure out some way you can listen and I can sleep.*
Type(s) of supportive language *description, problem orientation*

1. You're an adult child who moves back in with your parents. They say they expect you to follow the "rules of the house."

    Defense-arousing statement _____

    _____

    _____

    _____

    Type(s) of defensive language _____

    Supportive statement _____

    _____

    _____

    _____

Type(s) of supportive language _____

2. Your roommate tells you you're trying to be "somebody you're not."

Defense-arousing statement _____

_____

_____

_____

Type(s) of defensive language _____

Supportive statement _____

_____

_____

_____

Type(s) of supportive language _____

3. A boss criticizes you for being late for work when you've been having car trouble.

Defense-arousing statement _____

_____

_____

_____

Type(s) of defensive language _____

Supportive statement _____

_____

_____

_____

Type(s) of supportive language _____

4. An elderly in-law who lives across the country calls to tell you what a bad job you're doing raising your child.

Defense-arousing statement _____

_____

_____

_____

Type(s) of defensive language _____

Supportive statement _____

_____

_____

_____

Type(s) of supportive language _____

5. You are camping with your children. The people on the site next to you are partying loudly into the night, making it impossible for your children to sleep.

Defense-arousing statement _____

_____

_____

_____

Type(s) of defensive language _____

Supportive statement _____

_____

_____

_____

Type(s) of supportive language _____

6. On many occasions a friend drops by your place without calling first. Because you often have other plans, this behaviour puts you in an uncomfortable position.

Defense-arousing statement _____

_____

_____

_____

Type(s) of defensive language _____

Supportive statement _____

_____

_____

_____

Type(s) of supportive language _____

Record a situation of your own here.

7. _____

_____

Defense-arousing statement _____

_____

_____

_____

Type(s) of defensive language _____

Supportive statement _____

_____

_____

_____

Type(s) of supportive language _____

NAME _____

9.3 COPING WITH TYPICAL CRITICISM

❖ Activity Type: Skill Builder

PURPOSE
To help you practise nondefensive responses to typical criticisms you may face.

INSTRUCTIONS
1. For each situation below, write a nondefensive response you could use that follows the guidelines of seeking more information or agreeing with the critic, as described in Chapter 9 of *Looking Out/Looking In*.
2. Join with two partners and identify the members as A, B, and C.
3. Role-play situations 1 and 2 with A responding to the criticisms offered by B, while C uses the checklist from Activity 9.4 to evaluate A's behaviour.
4. Switch roles so that B responds to C's criticisms on items 3 and 4, while A completes the checklist.
5. Switch roles again so that C responds to A's criticisms on items 5 and 6, while B completes the checklist.
6. Repeat for remaining situations.

SITUATION	HOW I COULD RESPOND EFFECTIVELY TO THE CRITICISM
1. You've been late for work every day this week. Just who do you think you are that you can come wandering in after the rest of us are already working?	
2. This place is a mess! Don't you care about how we live?	
3. No wonder your grades are low. You're always out partying instead of studying.	
4. Your sister got terrific grades this term.	

SITUATION	HOW I COULD RESPOND EFFECTIVELY TO THE CRITICISM
5. How could you have been so thoughtless at the party last night?	
6. It takes you so long to get the idea.	
7. You think I'm your personal servant!	
8. Haven't you finished that yet?	
9. What's the matter with you? You've been so cold lately.	
10. Why can't your children be quiet like theirs?	
11. You should have consulted somebody before acting on that.	
12. Your motivation level sure is low lately.	

NAME _____

9.4   RESPONDING NONDEFENSIVELY

❖ Activity Type: Oral Skill

PURPOSE
To give you practice in responding nondefensively, in as realistic a situation as possible.

BACKGROUND
Although this exercise may seem somewhat dangerous, that isn't actually the case. The recipient of the criticism is in a position of strength because he or she is asking for the criticism as a way to build skills, as opposed to the usual way we receive criticism – through the back door!

INSTRUCTIONS
1.   Pair up with someone you know well and trust. This may be a class member, a friend, or a relative. Ideally, the person should have some creative acting potential.
2.   Have your partner come up with a criticism to level at you. He or she should be told to think of something that is either a real complaint, an embellishment on a minor criticism, or something completely made up but that sounds as if it could be real. The main point here is that you should not be able to figure out whether your partner is serious or not. Your partner likewise should not tell you if he or she is serious – unless you ask to be told at the end of the exercise. The other restriction here is that the criticism should focus on how you operate (as a friend, student, worker, etc.), not on physical appearance or other areas of a highly personal or sensitive nature.
3.   Ask your partner to level the "criticism" at you, while you practise the responding techniques in the checklist below.
4.   When you are finished, ask your partner whether at any point you seemed defensive. When? What did you do?
5.   Then explain to your partner the techniques in the checklist, and see how many he or she can identify from your responses.
6.   To conclude this exercise, you may, if you wish, ask your partner to tell you if he or she was serious about the criticism – it's completely up to you.

CHECKLIST
Seeks additional information to understand the critic/criticism better by

_____   Asking for details

_____   Guessing about specific details

_____   Paraphrasing to confirm understanding and encourage further discussion

_____   Asking what the critic wants/needs in this situation to make it better

_____   Asking the critic to describe the consequences of the behaviour for the critic

_____   Asking if anything else is wrong

Agrees, as appropriate, with the criticism as

_____   True factually

_____   Valid within the context of how the critic experienced the event (and as the critic's right to have a different perception)

Maintains appropriate verbal and nonverbal behaviours to indicate sincerity through

_____   Tone of voice

_____   Facial expressions

_____   Posture and gestures

_____   Body orientation and distance

NAME _____

9.5   MEDIATED MESSAGES—CLIMATE

❖ Activity Type: Group Discussion

PURPOSE
To apply the concept of communication climate to mediated contexts.

INSTRUCTIONS
Discuss each of the questions below in your group. Prepare written answers for your instructor, or be prepared to contribute to a large group discussion, comparing your experiences with those of others in your class.

1. Communication climate is the emotional tone of a relationship. Describe how the use of mediated forms of communication channels (e.g., telephone, e-mail) contributes to the communication climate of your relationships.

    _____

    _____

2. Simply receiving a call, letter, or e-mail from someone can make you feel supported. Compile a list of the ways we can use mediated messages to recognize, acknowledge, and endorse others.

    _____

    _____

3. Defensive spirals negatively reinforce ineffective patterns of communication. Give examples of how mediated messages have contributed to or helped minimize defensive spirals in your relationships.

    _____

    _____

4. Your textbook describes ways we can respond nondefensively to criticism. In which mediated contexts can this skill be used most effectively?

    _____

    _____

NAME _____

9.6   YOUR CALL—CLIMATE

❖ Activity Type: Group Discussion

PURPOSE
To analyze defensiveness in relationships.

INSTRUCTIONS
Use the case below and the discussion questions that follow to discuss the variety of communication issues involved in effective communication. Make notes on this page, add other pages on your own, or prepare a group report/analysis based on your discussion. Add your own experiences to individualize the analysis to make it "Your Call."

CASE
Gil and Lydia are brother and sister. They love one another and feel close. Their mother often tells Gil how lovely it is of Lydia to call her so often, how pretty Lydia is, what a good athlete she is, and how much she enjoys Lydia bringing home her friends to visit. Mother tells Lydia how smart Gil is, how hard he works, how many interesting things he does, and how well he manages money. The overall climate of the relationship between Gil and Lydia and their mother is good, but both Gil and Lydia find themselves getting defensive when their mother praises the other.

1. Why might Gil and Lydia get defensive about these positive statements?

   _____

   _____

2. Discuss situations similar to the one above, in which you and others in your group have reacted defensively to statements that, on the surface, are positive and supportive.

   _____

   _____

3. How might Gil or Lydia use the skills for coping with criticsm, as described in your textbook, to handle their defensiveness with their mother and one another?

   _____

   _____

4. If their mother knew about Gil's and Lydia's defensive reations, should she change the kinds of comments she makes about each sibling to the other one? What is her responsibility in this situation?

_____

_____

STUDY GUIDE

CROSSWORD PUZZLE

Across

2   a disconfirming response with more than one meaning, leaving the other party unsure of the responder's position

4   a defense mechanism in which a person stresses a strength in one area to camouflage a shortcoming in some other area

5   a disconfirming response that ignores another person's attempt to communicate

7   the emotional tone of a relationship between two or more individuals

9   communication messages that express caring or respect for another person

10 a verbal attack disguised as humour

11 a reciprocating communication pattern that reinforces the saying "what goes around comes around"

12 to block out dissonant information

13 categories of behaviours that arouse defensiveness of feelings of being respected

Down

1   a cognitive inconsistency between two conflicting pieces of information, attitudes, or behaviours

2   a defence mechanism in which a person avoids admitting emotional pain by pretending not to care about an event

3   a disconfirming response that implicitly or explicitly attributes responsibility for the speaker's displeasure to another party

6   communication messages that express a lack of caring or respect for another person

8   a defence mechanism in which a person vents hostile or aggressive feelings on a target that cannot strike back, instead of on the true target

9   communication in which the sender tries to impose some sort of outcome on the receiver, usually resulting in a defensive reaction

TRUE/FALSE

Mark the statements below as true or false. Correct statements that are false on the lines below to create a true statement.

_____   **1.**   The tone or climate of a relationship is shaped by the degree to which the people believe themselves to be valued by one another.

_____   **2.**   Disagreeing with another person is always disconfirming or defence-arousing.

_____   **3.**   Most experts agree that it is psychologically healthier to have someone ignore you than disagree with you.

_____   **4.**   Recognition communicates the highest form of valuing.

_____   **5.**   When the criticism levelled at us is accurate, we will not get defensive.

_____   **6.**   Communicators strive to resolve inconsistencies or conflicting pieces of information because this "dissonant" condition is uncomfortable.

_____ **7.** Using Jack Gibb's supportive behaviours will eliminate defensiveness in your receivers.

_____

_____ **8.** According to your text, spontaneity can sometimes be used as a strategy.

_____

_____ **9.** In order to cope with criticism, you should not express disagreement with the critic's perceptions.

_____

_____ **10.** In order to cope with criticism, you should not express disagreement with any of the critic's statements.

_____

COMPLETION

The Gibb categories of defensive and supportive behaviour are six sets of contrasting styles of verbal and nonverbal behaviour. Each set describes a communication style that is likely to arouse defensiveness and a contrasting style that is likely to prevent or reduce it. Fill in the blanks with the Gibb behaviour described chosen from the list below.

evaluation	description	control	problem orientation	strategy
spontaneity	neutrality	empathy	superiority	equality
certainty	provisionalism			

1. _____ is the attitude behind messages that imply there is no possibility of error on the part of the speaker.

2. _____ is communication behaviour involving messages that describe the speaker's position without evaluating others.

3. _____ is a supportive style of communication in which the communicators are interested in jointly finding ways to resolve an issue.

4. _____ is a defense-arousing style of communication in which the sender tries to manipulate or deceive a receiver.

5. _____ is a supportive style of communication in which the sender expresses a willingness to consider the other person's position.

6. _____ is a defence-arousing style of communication in which the sender communicates judgment of the receiver's thoughts or actions.

7. _____ is a supportive communication behaviour in which the sender expresses a message openly and honestly without any attempt to manipulate the receiver.

8. _____ is a defence-arousing behaviour in which the sender expresses indifference toward a receiver.

9. _____ is a defense-arousing message in which the sender tries to impose some sort of outcome on the receiver.

10. _____ is a type of supportive communication that suggests that the sender regards the receiver as worthy of respect.

MULTIPLE CHOICE

Choose the letter of the defensive or supportive category that is best illustrated by each of the situations below.

a. evaluation
b. control
c. strategy
d. neutrality
e. superiority
f. certainty

g. description
h. problem orientation
i. spontaneity
j. empathy
k. equality
l. provisionalism

_____ 1. Derek insists he has all the facts and needs to hear no more information.

_____ 2. Richard has a strong opinion but will listen to another position.

_____ 3. Lina kept looking at the clock as she was listening to Nan, so Nan thought Lina didn't consider her comments as very important.

_____ 4. "I know Arienne doesn't agree with me," Heidi said, "but she knows how strongly I feel about this, and I think she understands my position."

_____ 5. "Even though my professor has a Ph.D.," Rosa pointed out, "she doesn't act like she's the only one who knows something; she is really interested in what I have to say too."

_____ 6. "When I found out that Klaus had tricked me into thinking his proposal was my idea so I'd support it, I was really angry."

_____ 7. "Even though we *all* wait tables here, Evanne thinks she's better than any of us – just look at the way she prances around!"

_____ 8. Clara sincerely and honestly told Georgia about her reservations concerning Georgia's planned party.

_____ 9. The co-workers attempted to find a solution to the scheduling issue that would satisfy both of their needs.

_____ 10. "It seems as though my father's favourite phrase is 'I know what's best for you,' and that really drives me up the wall."

_____ 11. "You drink too much."

_____ 12. "I was embarrassed when you slurred your speech in front of my boss."

_____ 13. "The flowers and presents are just an attempt to get me to go to bed with him."

_____ **14.** "She looked down her nose at me when I told her I didn't exercise regularly."

_____ **15.** "It sounds like we both want something different. So where do we go from here?"

Choose the letter of the type of coping with criticism that is best illustrated by each of the situations below.

   a.   ask for specific details of criticism
   b.   guess about specific details
   c.   paraphrase to clarify criticism
   d.   ask what the critic wants
   e.   ask critic to describe the consequences of behaviour
   f.   ask what else is wrong
   g.   agree with true facts
   h.   agree with critic's right to perceive differently

Criticism: "You never seem to care about much."

_____ **16.** "Are you referring to my not going to the office party?"

_____ **17.** "You're right. I probably could have gotten more quotes for the job before going ahead with it."

_____ **18.** "How would you rather I handle situations like that in the future?"

_____ **19.** "I can see why you'd be upset with me for not going to the party, because you've told me you want me to be more involved with your work's social events."

_____ **20.** "When I didn't go to the party, were you embarrassed or something?"

_____ **21.** "So not calling you back right away was a problem. Have I upset you any other way?"

_____ **22.** "So you're upset that I'm not visiting you every week, and you think that shows a lack of affection on my part – is that it?"

_____ **23.** "What do you mean?"

_____ **24.** "I really do appreciate how it looked to you like none of us noticed how hard you were trying."

_____ **25.** "Because I wasn't at the party, it reflected badly on you?"

STUDY GUIDE ANSWERS

CROSSWORD PUZZLE

			¹d											
²a	m	b	i	g	u	o	u	s						
p			s											
a			s					³c						
t		⁴c	o	m	p	e	n	s	a	t	i	o	n	
h			n					m						
y			a					⁵i	m	p	e	r	v	i	o	u	s
			n	⁶d				l						
		⁷c	l	i	m	a	t	e						
		e		s				i		⁸d				
				c			⁹c	o	n	f	i	r	m	i	n	g
				o			o		i	s				
				n			n		n	p				
				f			t		g	l				
				i			r			¹⁰s	a	r	c	a	s	m
				r			o			c				
				m			l			e				
		¹¹s	p	i	r	a	l			m				
				n			i		¹²T	e	p	r	e	s	s
			¹³g	i	b	b	n			n				
							g			t				

TRUE/FALSE

1. T	**3.** F	**5.** F	**7.** F	**9.** T
2. F	**4.** F	**6.** T	**8.** T	**10.** F

COMPLETION

1. certainty
2. description
3. problem orientation
4. strategy
5. provisionalism
6. evaluation
7. spontaneity
8. neutrality
9. control
10. equality

MULTIPLE CHOICE

1. f	**6.** c	**11.** a	**16.** b	**21.** f
2. l	**7.** e	**12.** g	**17.** g	**22.** c
3. d	**8.** i	**13.** c	**18.** d	**23.** a
4. j	**9.** h	**14.** e	**19.** h	**24.** h
5. k	**10.** b	**15.** h	**20.** b	**25.** b

CHAPTER 10

Managing Interpersonal Conflicts

OUTLINE

Use this outline to take notes as you read the chapter in the text and/or as your instructor lectures in class.

I. The nature of conflict

A. Definition
1. Expressed struggle
2. Perceived incompatible goals
3. Perceived scarce rewards
4. Interdependence
5. Interference from the other party

B. Conflict Is Natural

C. Conflict Can Be Beneficial

II. Personal conflict styles

A. Nonassertive Behaviour
1. Avoidance
2. Accommodation

B. Direct Aggression

C. Passive Aggression—"Crazymaking"

D. Indirect Communication

E. Assertion

F. Determining the Best Style
1. Situation
2. Receiver
3. Your goals

III.   Assertion without aggression: The clear message format

A.   Behaviour

B.   Interpretation

C.   Feeling

D.   Consequence
1.   What happens to you, the speaker
2.   What happens to the person you're addressing
3.   What happens to others

E.   Intention
1.   Where you stand on an issue
2.   Requests of others
3.   Descriptions of how you plan to act in the future

F.   Using the Clear Message Format
1.   May be delivered in mixed order
2.   Word to suit your personal style
3.   Combine elements when appropriate
4.   Take your time delivering the message

IV.   Conflict in relational systems

A.   Complementary, Symmetrical, and Parallel Styles

B.   Intimate and Aggressive Styles

C.   Conflict Rituals

V.   Variables in conflict styles

A.   Gender

B.   Culture

VI.   Methods of conflict resolution

A.   Win–Lose

B.   Lose–Lose

C.   Compromise

D.   Win–Win

VII.   Win–win problem-solving skills

A.   Identify Your Problem and Unmet Needs

B.   Make a Date

C.   Describe Your Problem and Needs

D.   Consider Your Partner's Point of View

E.   **Negotiate a Solution**
   1.   Identify and define the conflict
   2.   Generate a number of possible solutions
   3.   Evaluate the alternative solutions
   4.   Decide on the best solution

F.   **Follow Up on the Solution**

VIII.   Constructive conflict: Questions and answers

A.   **Isn't Win–Win Too Good to Be True?**

B.   **Isn't Win–Win Too Elaborate?**

C.   **Isn't Win–Win Negotiating *Too* Rational?**

D.   **Is It Possible to Change Others?**

KEY TERMS

Use these key terms to review major concepts from your text. Write the definition for each key term in the space to the right.

accommodation _____

aggressive conflict style _____

assertion _____

avoidance _____

behavioural description _____

clear message format _____

complementary conflict style _____

compromise _____

conflict _____

conflict resolution _____

conflict ritual _____

consequence statement _____

crazymaking _____

direct aggression _____

feeling statement _____

indirect communication _____

indirect conflict style _____

intention statement _____

interdependence _____

interpretation _____

lose–lose problem solving _____

nonassertion _____

parallel conflict style _____

passive aggression _____

relational conflict style _____

scarce rewards _____

symmetrical conflict style _____

win–lose problem solving _____

win–win problem solving _____

NAME _____

ACTIVITIES

10.1   UNDERSTANDING CONFLICT STYLES

◆❖ Activity Type: Skill Builder

PURPOSE
To help you understand the styles with which conflicts can be handled.

INSTRUCTIONS
1. For each of the conflicts described, write five responses illustrating nonassertive, directly aggressive, passive-aggressive, indirect communication, and assertive communication styles.
2. Describe the probable consequences of each style.

EXAMPLE
Three weeks ago your friend borrowed an article of clothing, promising to return it soon. You haven't seen it since, and the friend hasn't mentioned it.

a. Nonassertive response *Say nothing to the friend, hoping she will remember and return the item.*
   Probable consequences *There's a good chance I'll never get the item back. I would probably resent the friend and avoid her in the future so I won't have to lend anything else.*

b. Directly aggressive response *Confront the friend and accuse her of being inconsiderate and irresponsible. Say that she probably ruined the item and is afraid to say so.*
   Probable consequences *My friend would get defensive and hurt. Even if she did intentionally keep the item, she'd never admit it when approached this way. We would probably avoid each other in the future.*

c. Passive-aggressive response *Complain to another friend, knowing it will get back to her.*
   Probable consequences *My friend might be embarrassed by my gossip and be even more resistant to returning it.*

d. Indirect communication *Drop hints about how I loved to wear the borrowed item. Casually mention how much I hate people who don't return things.*
   Probable consequences *My friend might ignore my hints. She'll most certainly resent my roundabout approach, even if she returns the article.*

e. Assertive response *Confront the friend in a noncritical way and remind her that she still has the item. Ask when she'll return it, being sure to get a specific time.*
   Probable consequences *The friend might be embarrassed when I bring the subject up, but because there's no attack it'll probably be okay. Since we'll have cleared up the problem, the relationship can continue.*

1. Someone you've just met at a party criticizes a mutual friend in a way you think is unfair.

   a.   Nonassertive response _____

   _____

   _____

   Probable consequences _____

   _____

   b.   Directly aggressive response _____

   _____

   _____

   Probable consequences _____

   _____

   c.   Passive-aggressive response _____

   _____

   _____

   Probable consequences _____

   _____

   d.   Indirect communication _____

   _____

   _____

   Probable consequences _____

   _____

   e.   Assertive response _____

   _____

   _____

   Probable consequences _____

   _____

2. The people sitting behind you at the cinema are talking about the movie just loud enough for you to be completely distracted and unable to enjoy the movie. There are no other good seats left either.

a.   Nonassertive response _____

_____

_____

Probable consequences _____

_____

b.   Directly aggressive response _____

_____

_____

Probable consequences _____

_____

c.   Passive-aggressive response _____

_____

_____

Probable consequences _____

_____

d.   Indirect communication _____

_____

_____

Probable consequences _____

_____

e.   Assertive response _____

_____

_____

Probable consequences _____

_____

5. Earlier in the day you asked the person with whom you live to stop by the store and pick up snacks for a party you are having this evening. Your roommate arrives home without the food, and it's too late to return to the store.

a.   Nonassertive response _____

_____

_____

Probable consequences _____

_____

b.   Directly aggressive response _____

_____

_____

Probable consequences _____

_____

c.   Passive-aggressive response _____

_____

_____

Probable consequences _____

_____

d.   Indirect communication _____

_____

_____

Probable consequences _____

_____

e.   Assertive response_____

_____

_____

Probable consequences _____

_____

4. You have been waiting your turn for what seems like forever at the cosmetics counter. You are running late already and getting frustrated. Just as a salesperson becomes available, another customer comes along and gets served immediately, as if you didn't exist.

   a. Nonassertive response _____

       _____

       _____

       Probable consequences _____

       _____

   b. Directly aggressive response _____

       _____

       _____

       Probable consequences _____

       _____

   c. Passive-aggressive response _____

       _____

       _____

       Probable consequences _____

       _____

   d. Indirect communication _____

       _____

       _____

       Probable consequences _____

       _____

   e. Assertive response _____

       _____

       _____

       Probable consequences _____

_____

5. You find out that a friend at work told other people with whom you work some very personal information about you.

a.   Nonassertive response _____

_____

_____

Probable consequences _____

_____

b.   Directly aggressive response _____

_____

_____

Probable consequences _____

_____

c.   Passive-aggressive response _____

_____

_____

Probable consequences _____

_____

d.   Indirect communication _____

_____

_____

Probable consequences _____

_____

e.   Assertive response_____

_____

_____

Probable consequences _____

NAME _____

10.2 WRITING CLEAR MESSAGES

◆❖ Activity Type: Skill Builder

PURPOSE
To help you turn unclear messages into clear ones.

INSTRUCTIONS
Imagine a situation in which you might have said each of the statements below. Rewrite the messages in the clear message format, being sure to include each of the five elements described in your text.

EXAMPLE

Unclear message: "It's awful when you can't trust a friend."

Clear message:

Lena, when I gave you the keys to my house so you could borrow those clothes   (behaviour)

I figured you'd know to lock up again when you left.   (interpretation)

I was worried and scared   (feeling)

because I found the door unlocked and thought there was a break-in.   (consequence)

I want to know if you left the house open, and let you know how upset I am.   (intention)

1. "Blast it, Anil! Get off my back."

   _____   (behaviour)

   _____   (interpretation)

   _____   (feeling)

   _____   (consequence)

   _____   (intention)

2. "I wish you'd pay more attention to me."

_____ (behaviour)

_____ (interpretation)

_____ (feeling)

_____ (consequence)

_____ (intention)

3. "You've sure been thoughtful lately."

_____ (behaviour)

_____ (interpretation)

_____ (feeling)

_____ (consequence)

_____ (intention)

4. "Nobody's perfect!"

_____ (behaviour)

_____ (interpretation)

_____ (feeling)

_____ (consequence)

_____ (intention)

5. "Matthias, you're such a slob!"

_____ (behaviour)

_____ (interpretation)

_____ (feeling)

_____ (consequence)

_____ (intention)

6. "Let's just forget it; with all the screaming, I get flustered."

_____ (behaviour)

_____ (interpretation)

_____ (feeling)

_____ (consequence)

_____ (intention)

7. "I really shouldn't eat any of that cake you baked."

_____ (behaviour)

_____ (interpretation)

_____ (feeling)

_____ (consequence)

_____ (intention)

Now list three significant messages that you could send to important people in your life: complaints, requests, or expressions of appreciation. Write them in clear message format.

8. _____ (behaviour)

_____ (interpretation)

_____ (feeling)

_____ (consequence)

_____ (intention)

9. _____ (behaviour)

_____ (interpretation)

_____ (feeling)

_____ (consequence)

_____ (intention)

10. _____ (behaviour)

_____ (interpretation)

_____ (feeling)

_____ (consequence)

_____ (intention)

NAME _____

10.3 YOUR CONFLICT STYLES

◆ Activity Type: Invitation to Insight

PURPOSE
To help you identify the styles you use to handle conflicts.

INSTRUCTIONS
1. Use the following form to record the conflicts that occur in your life. Describe any minor issues that arise, as well as major problems.
2. For each incident, describe your behaviour, your conflict style, your approach to resolution, and the consequences of this behaviour.
3. Summarize your findings in the space provided.

INCIDENT	YOUR BEHAVIOUR	YOUR CONFLICT STYLE	APPROACH TO RESOLUTION	CONSEQUENCES
EXAMPLE My friend accused me of being too negative about the possibility of finding rewarding, well-paying work.	I became defensive and angrily denied his claim. In turn I accused him of being too critical.	Direct aggression	Win–lose	After arguing for some time, we left each other, both feeling upset. I'm sure we'll both feel awkward around each other for a while.
1.				
2.				

INCIDENT	YOUR BEHAVIOUR	YOUR CONFLICT STYLE	APPROACH TO RESOLUTION	CONSEQUENCES
3.				
4.				
5.				

CONCLUSIONS

Are there any individuals or issues that repeatedly arouse conflicts?

_____

_____

_____

_____

What conflict style(s) do you most commonly use? Do you use different styles with different people or in different situations? Describe.

_____

_____

_____

_____

_____

_____

What approaches do you usually take in resolving conflicts? Do you use different approaches depending on the people or situations? Describe.

_____

_____

_____

_____

Are you satisfied with the consequences of the styles and approaches used? Why or why not?

_____

_____

_____

_____

NAME _____

10.4 THE ENDS VS. THE MEANS

◆❖ Activity Type: Invitation to Insight

PURPOSE
To help you distinguish the ends, and the means to those ends, in a personal conflict.

INSTRUCTIONS
1. In each of the following conflict situations, identify the *ends* each party seems to be seeking. There may be ends that the relationship shares, as well as individual ends for each of the parties involved. Ends in a conflict are the overall, general (often relational) goals that the dyad has.
2. Brainstorm a series of possible *means* that could achieve each person's (and the relationship's) ends. Means are the many possible ways to reach the end state.
3. Record conflict situations of your own, identifying ends and means.

CONFLICT SITUATION	SHARED ENDS	SPEAKER'S ENDS	OTHER'S ENDS	POSSIBLE MEANS
EXAMPLE My friend wants me to visit her in Vancouver and meet her family. I'd like to visit, but it would cost a lot, and I'd rather save the money for something else.	We both want to maintain the affection in the relationship. We both want each other to know we are important to each other and that we care about each other and our families.	I want to spend as little money as possible while still letting my friend know how important she is to me. I don't want to lose her friendship.	She wants to show her family what a good friend I am and have some companionship while she has to stay in Vancouver.	(1) She/her family send me money to go to Vancouver. (2) We share the costs. (3) I combine whatever else I want to do with a short trip to Vancouver. (4) We arrange for her family to meet me when they next come to our city. (5) My friend comes back with her sister or mother to spend time with me.
1. My roommate wants a friend (whom I dislike) to sublease a room in our apartment.				
2. I am dating a person who's of a different race than I am, and my family thinks this is a mistake.				

CONFLICT SITUATION	SHARED ENDS	SPEAKER'S ENDS	OTHER'S ENDS	POSSIBLE MEANS
3. My older sisters think, because of many alcohol problems in our family, that I'll turn into an alcoholic. I tell them not to worry, but they won't get off my back.				
4. My partner thinks I flirt too much.				
5. My mom keeps asking me about my grades and nagging me on the issue of my boyfriend. She thinks I'm going to make the same mistakes as she did.				

CONFLICT SITUATION	SHARED ENDS	SPEAKER'S ENDS	OTHER'S ENDS	POSSIBLE MEANS
6. Some people in my office enjoy listening to country music all the time. I've got nothing against it, but it gets old. I'd like more variety.				
7.				
8.				
9.				

NAME _____

10.5 WIN–WIN PROBLEM SOLVING

◆❖ Activity Type: Invitation to Insight

PURPOSE
To help you apply the win–win problem-solving method to a personal conflict.

INSTRUCTIONS
1. Follow the instructions below as a guide to dealing with an interpersonal conflict facing you now.
2. After completing the no-lose steps, record your conclusions in the space provided.

Step 1: Identify your unmet needs.

_____

_____

_____

_____

Step 2: Make a date. (Choose a time and place that will make it easiest for both parties to work constructively on the issue.)

_____

_____

_____

_____

Step 3: Describe your problem and needs. (Use behaviour – interpret – feel – consequence – intention format, but avoid proposing specific means or solutions at this point.)

_____

_____

_____

_____

Step 4: Ask your partner to show that s/he understands you (paraphrase or perception-check).

_____

_____

_____

_____

Step 5: Consider your partner's point of view. (Ask your partner what he or she wants and check your understanding; paraphrase or perception-check as necessary.)

_____

_____

_____

_____

Step 6: Negotiate a solution.

   a. Restate the needs of both parties, just to be sure they are clear.

_____

_____

_____

_____

   b. Work together to generate a number of possible solutions that might satisfy these needs. Don't criticize any suggestions here!

_____

_____

_____

_____

_____

_____

_____

c. Evaluate the solutions you just listed, considering the advantages and problems of each. If you think of any new solutions, record them above.

_____

_____

_____

d. Decide on the best solution and record it here.

_____

_____

_____

_____

Step 7: Follow up on the solution. After a trial period, meet with your partner and see if your agreement is satisfying both your needs. If not, return to step 3 and use this procedure to refine your solution.

_____

_____

_____

CONCLUSIONS

In what ways did this procedure differ from the way in which you usually deal with interpersonal conflicts?

_____

_____

_____

Was the outcome of your problem-solving session different from what it might have been if you had communicated in your usual style? How?

_____

_____

_____

In what ways can you use the no-lose methods in your interpersonal conflicts? With whom? On what issues? What kinds of behaviour will be especially important?

_____

_____

_____

NAME _____

10.6 CONFLICT RESOLUTION DYADS

❖ Activity Type: Oral Skill

PURPOSE
To develop your skills in using the assertive, win–win conflict resolution methods introduced in Chapter 10 of *Looking Out/Looking In.*

INSTRUCTIONS
1. Join with a partner and discuss conflicts from your lives. Choose one that would be suitable for a win–win conflict attempt. One of you will role-play a real-life partner.
2. Engage in the win–win conflict resolution methods introduced in Chapter 10 of *Looking Out/Looking In.* (You may use Activity 10.5 to help you prepare this conflict.)
3. Use the checklist below to evaluate your performance (or videotape the conflict dyad and evaluate each other's performance).
4. On a separate sheet of paper describe how this method can be effectively and realistically applied to everyday conflicts.

CHECKLIST
5 = Superior   4 = Excellent   3 = Good   2 = Fair   1 = Poor

Sets a "date" for discussing the issue _____

Describes unmet needs to partner
  other's behaviour _____
  your interpretations _____
  your feelings _____
  consequences (for self and/or other) _____
  intentions _____

Seeks verification that partner understands statement of needs _____

Solicits partner's needs, as appropriate _____

Actively listens/perception-checks to verify understanding of partner's needs _____

Negotiates win–win solution to best possible extent _____
  identifies/summarizes conflict _____
  generates possible solutions without criticizing _____
  evaluates alternatives _____
  decides on win–win solution _____

Plans follow-up meeting to modify solution as necessary _____

                            Total _____

NAME _____

10.7 MEDIATED MESSAGES—CONFLICT MANAGEMENT

❖ Activity Type: Group Discussion

PURPOSE
To manage conflict in mediated contexts.

INSTRUCTIONS
Discuss each of the questions below in your group. Prepare written answers for your instructor, or be prepared to contribute to a large group discussion, comparing your experiences with those of others in your class.

1. Conflict is natural in relationships. Based on your experience, what is the likelihood of conflicts taking place when communication occurs in mediated contexts (e.g., e-mail, instant messaging/chat, telephone, and hard copy)? What are the pros and cons of managing conflict using mediated communication channels?

   _____

   _____

   _____

2. The clear message format could be used more easily in written communication (letters, e-mail); that is, you could have time to review/rewrite before sending the message. Describe the other advantages/disadvantages of the clear message format in each of the following channels: face-to-face, e-mail, instant messaging/chat, telephone, and hard copy (e.g., written notes, "snail mail").

   _____

   _____

   _____

3. Brainstorming is an important aspect of win–win problem solving. Discuss how mediated communication channels might help or hinder this process.

   _____

   _____

   _____

NAME _____

10.8   YOUR CALL — CONFLICT MANAGEMENT

❖ Activity Type: Group Discussion

PURPOSE
To apply conflict management principles to a relationships.

INSTRUCTIONS
Use the case below and the discussion questions that follow to discuss the variety of communication issues involved in effective communication. Make notes on this page, add other pages on your own, or prepare a group report/analysis based on your discussion. Add your own experiences to individualize the analysis to make it "Your Call."

CASE
Klaus and Drew have been roommates for two years, and they have had very few problems. But this term, Klaus has a difficult and early class schedule, and he has taken on more hours at work to make ends meet. Drew's parents support him completely, and he has a very light schedule this term. Klaus and Drew's friends continue to come to their house to party, and Drew is very irritated with Klaus because he's always studying and is a big bore all of a sudden. Klaus thinks Drew is a spoiled brat and insensitive to his needs. Neither Klaus nor Drew has said anything at this point.

1. Should Klaus and Drew bring this conflict out in the open? Would airing their differences be beneficial or harmful to the relationship?

   _____

   _____

2. Prepare clear messages for Klaus and Drew to give each other. Then evaluate whether they should deliver them or not.

   _____

   _____

3. What are the unmet needs of Klaus and Drew in this situation? Should they keep those unmet needs to themselves (be unassertive), or should they use one of the other personal conflict styles described in Chapter 10 of *Looking Out/Looking In*?

   _____

   _____

4. Could Klaus and Drew use the win–win problem-solving method outlined in your textbook? Describe why you think it would/would not work.

_____

_____

STUDY GUIDE

CROSSWORD PUZZLE

Across

3 an indirect expression of hostility, delivered in a way that allows the sender to maintain a façade of kindness

5 a nonassertive response style in which the communicator submits to a situation rather than attempt to have his or her needs met

8 an expressed struggle between at least two interdependent parties who perceive incompatible goals, scarce rewards, and interference

9 communication that is an oblique way of expressing wants or needs in order to save face for the recipient

12 a relational conflict style in which partners use different but mutually reinforcing behaviours

15 an approach to conflict resolution in which both parties end up disatisfied with the outcome

Down

1 the inability to express one's thoughts or feelings when necessary

2 when this is combined with aggression, the result is a relationship characterized by times of intense conflict as well as times of intense harmony

4 a relational conflict style in which both partners use the same tactics

6 an approach to conflict resolution in which both parties attain at least part of what they wanted through self-sacrifice

7 a nonassertive response style in which the communicator acts as if there were no conflict when one presents itself

9 a statement that describes where the speaker stands on an issue, what he or she wants, or how he or she plans to act in the future

10 a statement that explains the results that follow either from the behaviour of the person to whom the message is addressed or from the speaker's interpretation of the addressee's behaviour

11 a conflict style that is a pattern of managing disagreements that repeats itself over time in a relationship

13 a relational conflict style in which the approach of the partners varies from one situation to another

14 an unacknowledged repeating pattern of interlocking behaviour used by participants in a conflict

TRUE/FALSE

Mark the statements below as true or false. Correct statements that are false on the lines below to create a true statement.

_____ **1.** A conflict can exist only when both parties are aware of a disagreement.

_____

_____ **2.** It's better to establish only one or two good conflict rituals in a relationship so that each person knows what is expected of him or her when a dispute arises.

_____

_____ **3.** Very close and compatible relationships will not experience conflict.

_____

_____ **4.** The terms "conflict resolution" and "problem solving" are identical in meaning.

_____

_____ **5.** Nonassertion is always a bad idea.

_____

_____ **6.** Verbally abusive couples report significantly less relational satisfaction than do partners who communicate about their conflicts in other ways.

_____

_____ **7.** Satisfied conflict partners tend to make more complaints about personal characteristics than about behaviours.

_____

_____ **8.** Crazymaking is just another name for passive aggression.

_____

_____ **9.** "It takes two to tango" – in conflict, as in dancing, men and women behave in similar ways.

_____

_____ **10.** The most important cultural factor in shaping attitudes toward conflict is gender.

_____

COMPLETION

Fill in the blanks with the crazymaker term described below.

avoiders	pseudoaccommodators	guiltmakers	withholders	crisis ticklers
mind readers	trivial tyrannizers	gunnysackers	beltliners	trappers

1. _____ don't respond immediately when they get angry. Instead, they let conflicts build up until they all pour out at once.

2. _____ do things they know will irritate their conflict partner rather than honestly sharing their resentments.

3. _____ engage in character analyses, explaining what the other person *really* means, instead of allowing the other person to express feelings honestly.

4. _____ set up a desired behaviour for their partners, and then when the behaviour is met, they attack the very thing they requested.

5. _____ refuse to fight by leaving, falling asleep, or pretending to be busy.

6. _____ try to make their partners feel responsible for causing their pain even though they won't come right out and say what they feel or want.

7. _____ agree to go along with the other person's wishes but with no intention of actually following through.

8. _____ use intimate knowledge of their partners to get them "where it hurts."

9. _____ drop little pointed comments without actually saying what's bothering them.

10. _____ keep something of value from the other person rather than openly expressing their anger..

MULTIPLE CHOICE

Identify which element of a clear message is being used in each statement according to the key below:

a. behavioural description
b. interpretation
c. feeling
d. consequence
e. intention

_____ 1. I thought you meant it.

_____ 2. I'm worried about this course.

_____ 3. Now I'm not sure you even tried to find it.

_____ 4. I want to talk to you about the $20 you borrowed.

_____ 5. You haven't said much.

_____ 6. I don't know whether you're serious or not.

_____ 7. I'm worried too.

_____ 8. Ever since then I've found myself avoiding you.

_____ 9. I'm sorry you didn't like my work.

_____ 10. I want you to know how important this is to me.

_____ 11. It looks to me like you meant to embarrass me.

_____ 12. After the party at Art's, you seemed to withdraw.

_____ 13. I see you're wearing my ring again.

_____ 14. From now on you can count on me.

_____ **15.** I've never heard you swear before.

_____ **16.** . . . and since then I've been sleeping at my dad's house.

_____ **17.** Because that occurred, they won't work overtime.

_____ **18.** You made that remark about teachers being so rigid.

_____ **19.** I got really concerned then.

_____ **20.** I don't think I can take it much longer.

Choose the letter of the personal conflict style that is best illustrated by the behaviour found below.

  a. avoidance
  b. accommodation
  c. direct aggression
  d. assertion
  e. indirect communication
  f. passive aggression

_____ **21.** Every time I bring up the idea of children, Duncan starts talking about work.

_____ **22.** "I can't believe you were so stupid as to have erased the disk."

_____ **23.** Even though he wanted to go to the party, Hugo stayed home with Selina rather than hear her complain about how much he goes out.

_____ **24.** By mentioning how allergic she was to smoke, Genevieve hoped that her guest would smoke outside.

_____ **25.** "When you smoke inside, I start to cough and my eyes water, so please go out on the balcony when you want to smoke."

_____ **26.** Rather than tell Nick about his frustration over Nick's not meeting the deadline, Howard complained to others about Nick's unreliability while maintaining a smiling front to Nick.

_____ **27.** Carol wouldn't answer the phone after their disagreement because she was afraid it would be Nancy on the other end.

_____ **28.** Faced with his obvious distress, Nikki put her very important work aside to listen to him.

_____ **29.** Even though Nikki could see Kham's distress, she told him she had a deadline to meet in one hour and asked if they could talk then.

_____ **30.** (Sarcastically) "Oh, sure, I *loved* having dinner with your parents instead of going to the party Saturday night."

STUDY GUIDE ANSWERS

CROSSWORD PUZZLE

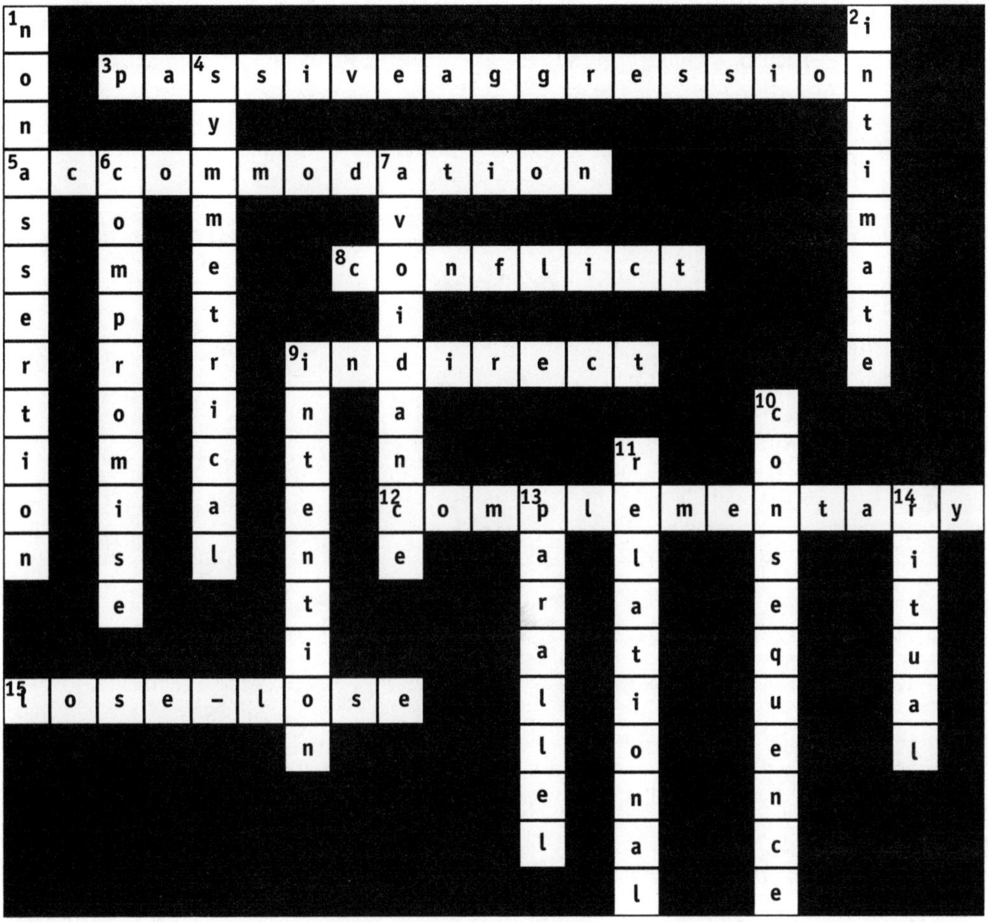
1 nonassertion
2 intimate
3 passiveaggression
4 symmetrical
5 accommodation
6 compromise
7 avoidance
8 conflict
9 indirect
intention
10 consequence
11 relational
12 complementary
13 parallel
14 ritual
15 lose-lose

TRUE/FALSE

1. T	**3.** F	**5.** F	**7.** F	**9.** F
2. F	**4.** F	**6.** T	**8.** T	**10.** F

COMPLETION

1. gunnysackers
2. trivial tyrannizers
3. mind readers
4. trappers
5. avoiders
6. guiltmakers
7. pseudoaccommodators
8. beltliners
9. crisis ticklers
10. withholders

MULTIPLE CHOICE

1.	b	**7.**	c	**13.**	a	**19.**	c	**25.**	d
2.	c	**8.**	d	**14.**	e	**20.**	e	**26.**	f
3.	b	**9.**	c	**15.**	a	**21.**	a	**27.**	a
4.	e	**10.**	e	**16.**	d	**22.**	c	**28.**	b
5.	a	**11.**	b	**17.**	d	**23.**	b	**29.**	d
6.	b	**12.**	b	**18.**	a	**24.**	e	**30.**	f